Christian Epp

Internet based Technologies and Systems for the support o. .... procurement

Bibliographic information published by the German National Library:

The German National Library lists this publication in the National Bibliography; detailed bibliographic data are available on the Internet at http://dnb.dnb.de .

Copyright © 1999 Diplomica Verlag GmbH
Print and binding: Books on Demand GmbH, Norderstedt Germany
ISBN: 9783838640105

http://www.diplom.de/e-book/219645/internet-based-technologies-and-systems-for-the-support-of-indirect-procurement

Christian Epp

Internet based Technologies and Systems for the support of indirect procurement

Diplom.de

Christian Epp

Internet based Technologies and Systems for the support of indirect procurement

Diplomarbeit
an der Universität Kaiserslautern
Fachbereich Wirtschaft
6 Monate Bearbeitungsdauer
März 1999 Abgabe

Diplom.de

Diplomica GmbH
Hermannstal 119 k
22119 Hamburg

Fon: 040 / 655 99 20
Fax: 040 / 655 99 222

agentur@diplom.de
www.diplom.de

ID 4010
Epp, Christian: Internet based Technologies and Systems for the support of indirect
procurement
Hamburg: Diplomica GmbH, 2001
Zugl.: Kaiserslautern, Universität, Diplomarbeit, 1999

Diplomica GmbH
http://www.diplom.de, Hamburg 2001
Printed in Germany

Table of Content

V

List of Figures

Abbreviations

APS .... Advanced Planning Scheduling
BOM .... Bill of Materials
DPS .... Desktop Purchasing Systems
EDI .... Electronic Data Interchange
EFT............... Electronic Funds Transfer
ERP .... Enterprise Resource Planning
FTP................ File Transfer Protocol
GE .... General Electric
GEIS............. General Electric (GE) Information Services
HTML........... Hyper Text Markup Language
HTTP .... Hyper Text Transfer Protocol
IAC .... Internet Application Components
IBTS .... Internet based Technologies and Systems
IP .... Internet Protocol
ISP................ Internet Service Provider
IT .... Information Technology
JIT .... Just in Time
MRO .... Maintenance, Repair, and Operating
MRP.............. Material Requirements Planning
MRP II........... Manufacturing Resource Planning
OBI .... Open Buying on the Internet
ORM .... Operating Resources Management
OTP.............. Open Trading Protocol
P-Card .... Procurement Card
P.O. .... Purchase Order
RAM.............. Random Access Memory
RFP .... Request for Proposals
RFQ.............. Request for Quotes
ROI .... Return on investment
SGML .... Standard Generalized Markup Language
SLA............... Software License Agreement
SOW .... Statement of Work
TCP .... Transport Control Protocol
TCO.............. Total Cost of Ownership
TPN .... Trading Process Network
TQM .... Total Quality Management
TVO .... Total Value of Ownership
VAN .... Value Added Network
WWW .... World Wide Web
XML .... eXtensible Markup Language

1 Introduction

1.1 Motivation

The "information technology revolution" has left virtually no area of business untouched. This revolution has seen significant advances in the procurement function of an organization in the ability to automate and systemize mundane and repetitive tasks [Bouv1995, p. 255].

Procurement is a business function that is performed in all enterprises. It is responsible for obtaining goods and services at the right price, in the right quantity, of the right quality, at the right time, from the right source with delivery at the right location [Watt 1995, p. 3, Zens1994, p. 6].

Purchases of goods and services are the largest single cost item in most companies. More dollar are spent for purchases of goods and services than for all other expense items combined, including wages, salaries, taxes, dividends, and depreciation [Kill1997, p. 5 - 17]. In addition, savings attained in purchasing translate dollar-for-dollar into profits. Because of that, reducing purchasing costs has a significant potential to improve the overall performance of an organization.

Until recently, research in procurement has mainly focused on the purchasing of direct goods, that is items that become part of the finished product. In this field, supply chain management strategies (including MRP, ERP, and EDI) aim to automate, manage and streamline the supply chain of key production materials. These systems are targeted especially to support the buying professional.

Depending on the type of industry and company, direct goods however constitute for only 40% of the total spend for goods and services. The remaining 60% are expenditures on "indirect" goods and services, which are items that do not become part of the finished product. These include items such as capital equipment, computer equipment and software, office supplies, maintenance, repair and operations (MRO) items and all types of services [Kill1997, p17]. The request of these items is usually initiated decentralized by any end-user

1

requisitioner within a company. This type of procurement has been neglected as a research field and has received little attention for efficiency gains even though it is characterized by being costly, time-consuming and inefficient.

Emerging technologies, especially Internet related Technologies have the potential to trigger significant changes in the field of indirect procurement.

First movers are already beginning to embrace new technologies and systems to support the procurement of indirect goods and services. Most of these systems concentrate on reducing the cost of processing a purchase order (transaction cost) by automating the procurement process. Early users hope to reduce the cost of processing a purchase order from currently estimated $80, down to $6 per purchase order. Therefore, they are especially suitable for the high volume, low cost items which usually account for roughly two-thirds of the purchase orders processed and only 3% of the dollars spent [Kill1997, p. 2]. However, these systems address only a subset of the entire range of indirect goods and services.

The objective in this thesis is to show how Internet based Technologies and Systems can support the procurement of the entire range of indirect goods and services.

1.2 Methodology

This thesis was written at the Fisher Center for Management & Information Technology, which is part of the Haas School of Business during a stay at the University of California at Berkeley. To develop this thesis guidance was provided by Prof. Arie Segev and Dr. Judith Gebauer of the Fisher Center.

Recent literature, trade journals, and Internet articles concerning the subject of procurement have been the main data basis for this thesis. In addition, information was captured from attending several forums on indirect procurement organized by the Fisher Center. Presentations of software vendors & integrators and first movers as well as discussions with attending procurement specialists provided further insights.

2

Further studies on the impact of Internet based technologies and systems on indirect procurement are being realized at the Fisher Center. This involves research on vendor systems and Internet technologies that go beyond this thesis.

1.3 Organization

The objective of this thesis is to show if and how Internet based Technologies and Systems are able to support the procurement of indirect goods and services. In order to do so, different procurement types are identified in chapter 2 and analyzed more in detail in chapter 3. Furthermore, Internet based Technologies and Systems are introduced in chapter 4.

These three chapters provide the bases for chapter 5 in which the matching between different procurement types and Internet based Technologies and Systems is realized. Figure 1 provides an overview of the organization of this thesis.

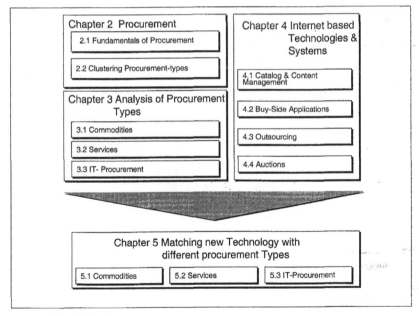

Figure 1: Roadmap

Chapter 2 introduces the fundamentals of procurement and purchasing beginning with a definition and evolution of procurement. Afterwards procurement is differentiated into direct and indirect procurement, with the focus being on the latter. This section ends with a clustering model that allows to identify different types of indirect procurement.

In chapter 3, some of these procurement types (commodities, services and IT-procurement) are addressed more in detail showing the "traditional" way of purchasing indirect goods and services. The main idea is to depict the procurement process and to identify the special user requirements of each procurement type

The objective in chapter 4 is to present the business model and main idea of the most promising and comprehensive Internet based Technologies and Systems that are able to (or have the potential to) support the procurement of indirect goods and services. Besides Catalog & Content Management, Buy-Side Applications such as Desktop Purchasing Systems (DPS) and Enterprise Resource Planning (ERP) systems, as well as Outsourcing and Auctions are going to be addressed.

In chapter 5 each of the identified procurement types is analyzed in respect of the possible support that Internet based Technologies and Systems are able to provide. In case that support is provided, the organizational implications and changes as well as some strength and weaknesses are depict.

2 Identify different types of indirect procurement

Since the focus of this thesis is to show how Internet-based technology and systems can support the procurement of indirect goods and services, special attention has to be given to the differences in the procurement process of the items purchased. These differences will determine what kind of functionality is needed from Internet-based technologies and systems in order to support that type of purchase. Therefore the objective in this chapter is to identify different procurement types which have the same requirements to the procurement processes.

This chapter begins with a brief introduction to the fundamentals of procurement and purchasing (see section 2.1). Afterwards procurement is differentiated into direct and indirect procurement, with the focus being on the latter. This section ends with a clustering model that allows identifying different types of indirect procurement which ideally have the same procurement process and the same requirements (see section 2.2).

2.1 Fundamentals of Procurement and Purchasing

The definitions of the terms purchasing and procurement vary in literature as well as throughout business organizations. Often, although somewhat imprecisely, these term are used interchangeably [Dobl1996, p.3]. In the following, some common definitions of both purchasing and procurement will be introduced:

- **Procurement** includes all activities involved in obtaining material, transporting them and moving them towards the production process [Zenz1993, p.5]. It tends to describe a broader and more proactive function than is commonly associated with purchasing by putting a stronger emphasis on strategic matters.

- **Purchasing** on the other hand is the act of buying goods and services and therefore represents a core element of procurement [Niss1996; Geba1996]. It is usually defined as the buying function of an organization and includes the acquisition of goods and services used in the operation of an organization. It is one of the basic functions common to all types of business enterprises [Dobl1996, 3; Fear1993, p5].

Regardless of the terminology differences depict, both terms are going to be used interchangeable throughout this thesis.

2.1.1 Purchasing Objectives and Organization

Like any other function of an organization, purchasing (procurement) is characterized by certain objectives. In general, purchasing is concerned to buy goods and services at the right price, in the right quantity, of the right quality, at the right time, from the right source with delivery at the right location [Watt1995, p.3; Chad1995, pp. 169-171; Zens1994, p. 9]

In practice the purchasing department can rarely fulfill them all equally because conflicts exist between some of the objectives. Usually some trade-offs must be made and therefore purchasing personnel seek a reasonable balance among them.

Furthermore, since purchasing is a **service organization** that exists primarily to meet the needs of other business functions, the objectives of procurement are closely related to the objectives of other departments in the enterprise, such as total quality management (TQM) and just-in-time (JIT). Therefore the procurement process not only has to meet multiple objectives simultaneously but also needs to establish, maintain, and balance a variety of external and internal relationships at the same time. [see Fear1993, p.9-12; Cart1995, pp.14-16; Perl1990, pp. 121-122].

As a service organization, purchasing is positioned between the company's **"internal customers"** in need of material to fulfill their tasks, and **external suppliers** providing goods and services [Hein1991, p. 17].

6

An oversimplified representation of this position between "internal customers" and external supplier is shown in Figure 2.

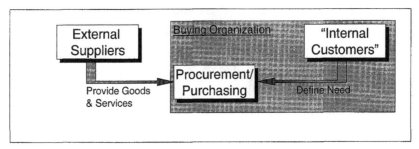

Figure 2: Procurement – a service organization

2.1.2 Procurement Evolution and Development

Traditionally, purchasing operated as a stand-alone function and its activities were confined to receiving material requests from user department and translating these into purchase orders or other contractual relationships with suppliers. As a result, in the past, purchasing was a reactive, paperwork and procedurally dominated function (Clerical Function), which focused basically on efficient transaction processing. In this relatively stable and transparent environment, purchasing decision making was of a repetitive and routine nature. The purchasing decisions were fairly well programmed and mainly addressed short-term operational issues [Keou1993, pp. 41-50].

In recent years, however, purchasing has undergone a change from an operational function to a more strategic one. The contemporary philosophy of purchasing's role is almost diametrically opposed to the "traditional" view. In the new strategic model, purchasing's role is to manage the process, rather than merely process its transactions. Decision making is based on long term multiple objectives, and instead of reacting to change, purchasing anticipates change and acts proactively [Kral93, pp.109-117].

Influenced by this transition from operational towards strategic procurement, organizations began to introduce electronic procurement applications since the nineteen sixties. These applications evolved into today's Manufacturing Resource Planning (MRP) and Enterprise Resource Planning (ERP) systems and focus specifically on automating the procurement of direct goods, that is, goods that become part of the finished product. They typically reward only the largest industrial companies, because they are fairly costly to implement and will return a positive ROI (Return on inverstment) only after large volumes are attained [Kill1997, p.1].

Most of these business-to-business electronic commerce systems (MRP, ERP) focus only on a fraction of the total goods and services a company purchases. They focus primarily on automating direct procurement. Therefore the remaining component of a company's spend, the entire range of indirect goods and services, that is goods and services that don't become part of the finished product, has not been automated yet. Until recently, it is an area that long has been neglected as a research field and received little attention for efficiency gains [Kill1997, p.3].

Nevertheless, new Internet-related technology has the potential to trigger significant changes in this long neglected area of procurement [Sege1998 August, p. 1]. A few early movers are already beginning to adopt this technology to streamline the procurement of indirect goods and services, which currently represents the latest stage in procurement evolution.

The following figure offers an overview of the above depict evolution of procurement. It shows the transition of purchasing's role from a clerical function, to a strategic business function and highlights the fact that procurement automation has occurred primarily in the area of direct procurement with such systems as EDI, ERP, and MRP. Only recently, Internet-related Technology is being used to support the procurement of indirect goods and services.

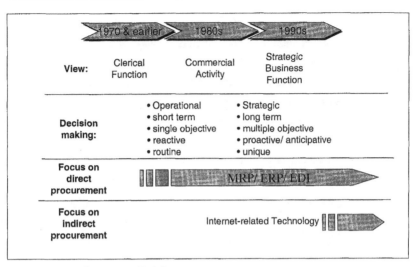

View:	Clerical Function	Commercial Activity	Strategic Business Function
Decision making:		• Operational • short term • single objective • reactive • routine	• Strategic • long term • multiple objective • proactive/ anticipative • unique
Focus on direct procurement		MRP/ ERP/ EDI	
Focus on indirect procurement		Internet-related Technology	

Figure 3: Procurement Evolution

Since the focus in this thesis is to show how Internet-based-Technologies and Systems can be used to support this long neglected field of procurement, it is important to get better understanding of the wide variety of items that make up the group of indirect goods and services.

First, however, it makes sense to understand the differences between direct and indirect procurement.

2.1.3 Direct and indirect procurement

The definition of direct and indirect procurement refers to the context of use in an organization [Färb1998, pp. 14-15].

• The procurement of raw materials, components, and parts used to compose the finished product is called **direct procurement**. Consequently, the goods that are purchased are called "direct goods". As depict before, this type of procurement has been automated by electronic procurement systems such as EDI, ERP, and MRP and is performed by professional buyers.

9

- The procurement of all other goods and services is called **indirect procurement** and the purchased items are called "indirect goods and services". This definition encompasses a wide range of different goods and services that are purchased by an organization. It includes items such as office supplies, services, and capital equipment. A more detailed view of the goods and services that make up the group of indirect procurement will be introduced in section 2.1.4. In contrast to direct procurement, usually everybody within an organization is requesting this type of items. Therefore the request originates decentralized throughout an organization.

Often the terms **production-oriented** and **non-production oriented** are used interchangeably with direct and indirect. However, they imply a slightly different meaning. For instance, production machines or lubricant oil can be considered as production-oriented, but both are indirect items because they are not part of the finished product [Färb1998, pp. 14-15].

The definition of direct and indirect procurement can best be applied in the context of industrial organizations where physical goods are used to compose a finished product. In service organizations, such as the financial service industry for instance, all procurement is indirect. Therefore, as opposed to direct procurement, indirect procurement is done in all industries [Färb1998, pp. 14-15].

Depending on the type of industry and company, purchases of goods and services (direct and indirect procurement) are the largest single cost item in most companies; larger than the combination of salaries and wages, taxes and profit. Figure 4 shows an average allocation of a company's sales dollar based on a composite of manufacturing, service and government organizations [Kill1997, p. 5].

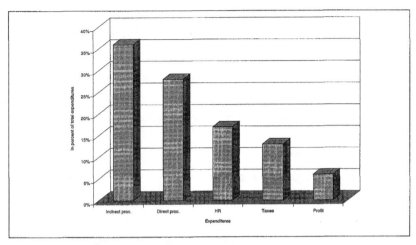

Figure 4: Average allocation of a company's sales dollar

As seen from the above figure, the average total indirect procurement spending usually outreaches the expenditures for direct procurement (depending on the type of industry and company). In the manufacturing industry usually 40 % of all expenditures on goods and services constitute for the purchase of direct goods, while up to 60 % of the expenditures are for indirect goods and services [Kill1997, p. 17]. Especially in the service sector, the share of indirect procurement is even higher and can be up to 100% (e.g., financial services) [Färb1998, pp. 14-15].

Taking into account that most of the electronic procurement systems mentioned before (ERP, MRP, EDI) have been aimed at making the purchasing of direct goods more streamlined and cost-efficient (see previous section: Evolution of procurement), it becomes clear that only a subset of the entire spend on goods and services has been optimized yet. In fact, in average only 40 % of the goods and services purchased by a company are covered and automated by these systems. Consequently, an average of 60 % of all goods and services (all indirect procurement) is left out of the equation and has received little attention for efficiency gains. Since cost savings attained in purchasing translate dollar-for-

11

dollar to an increase in profits, optimizing this type of procurement can have a measurable impact on the companies overall performance.

Now that the differences between direct and indirect procurement have been explained and the impact and potential of cost savings in the area of indirect procurement has been depict, it is important to focus more in detail on the actual items the make up the group of indirect goods and services.

2.1.4 Indirect Goods and Services

Indirect goods and services comprise a wide variety of items. They range from standardized low value items like most office supplies to complex and costly services like consulting.

In order to get an overview and better understanding of the diversity of items that make up indirect procurement, it is useful to categorize items. Therefore, some in purchasing literature presented categories of indirect procurement will be introduced first.

Purchasing literature usually deals with the procurement of indirect goods and services as a side issue. It usually distinguishes between three types of indirect items [Färb1998, p. 23]:

(1) maintenance, repair, and operating (MRO) supplies,

(2) capital equipment, and

(3) services.

The term MRO has a very narrow meaning. It is particularly common in manufacturing, but does not hold for many other industries such as financial services or the natural resources industry. Manufacturing uses the term MRO to describe goods, "which are consumed in the production process but which do not become part of the product (e.g., lubricating oil, soap, machine repair parts)" [Dob1996, p. 519].

The above introduced categories do not cover the entire range of indirect goods and services. The procurement of office supplies, for example, cannot be associated with any of these groups [Färb1998, pp. 23-24].

Aspect Development, a vendor of business-to-business electronic commerce solutions, tries to solve this **terminology problem** by extending the definition of MRO. They categorizes MRO into two groups [Färb1998, pp. 23-24]:

- *Office & administrative MRO* consisting of office supplies and office equipment, and

- *Manufacturing MRO*, consisting of plant & equipment and industrial & safety supplies [see Aspe1998, pp. 4-5].

Another approach to classify indirect procurement is presented by Killen & Associates. They introduce the term "operating resources" imbuing the handling of indirect goods and services with the same strategic status as the handling of manufacturing resources (direct goods). Operating resources can be defined as "goods and services that the company purchases to enable the continued operation of the company" [Kill1997, p. 3]. Figure 5 lists examples for operating resources [Kill1997, p. 5]. The definition of Killen & Associates covers the entire range of indirect goods and services and is yet only another way to categorize indirect procurement.

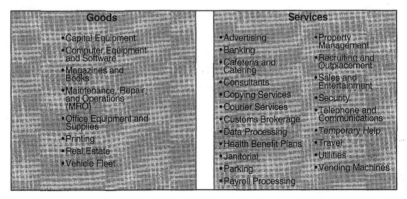

Figure 5: Examples for Operating Resources (Source: Färb1998, p. 24)

The above-presented approaches are useful to get a better understanding about the wide range of goods and services that make up the group of indirect procurement. Since their main focus is to cover the entire range of goods and services, they differ among each other only because they use **different terminology's** to categorize indirect procurement. Non-of the approaches place the procurement process of indirect goods and services into their focal point to come up with a categorization. Therefore, they don't consider the differences that exist in the procurement process, even though they might be quit significant for this wide range of items, depending on variables such as the dollar value of an item or the frequency of transaction, among others.

Requirements concerning the procurement process of low dollar standardized products that are purchased on a daily basis are very different from those items that are of high value and purchased only once. The purchase of services is very different from the purchase of physical goods and even within the service procurement the requirements can vary widely. The procurement of janitorial services is very different than the procurement of consulting services. Consequently, the procurement process and the required procurement systems able to support this wide range of items can not be the same.

The following figure may help to explain this fact. Two exemplary items with diametrically opposed characteristics are presented to show how these characteristics determine certain requirements to the procurement process. These requirements need to be addressed by a procurement system that aims at supporting the procurement process.

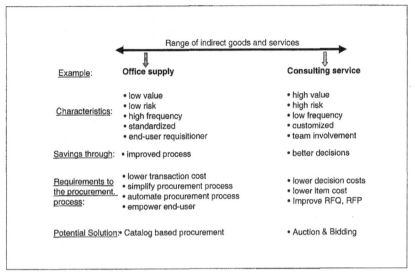

Figure 6: Range of goods and services

Since the focus of this thesis is to show how Internet-based technology and systems can support the procurement of indirect goods and services, special attention has to be given to the different characteristics of an item purchased. These characteristics determine the requirements to the procurement process and consequently decide upon what kind of functionality is needed from Internet-based Technologies and Systems in order to support that type of purchase.

As shown before, there seems to be no approach in literature that is really useful for this thesis. Therefore a possible way to cluster the wide range of indirect goods and services into different types of procurement, which have similar procurement processes and requirements, will be presented in the following. This will allow to find Internet-based Solutions that are targeted to address the special requirements of each procurement-type.

2.2 Clustering different types of procurement

As shown in the previous section, not all indirect goods and services are purchased the same way. Many products require special knowledge and many things need to be considered for one type of purchase, which do not apply to another. The purchasing process varies widely according to the characteristics of the items purchased [Houg1992, p. 297].

This section will serve to identify different types of procurement. The objective is not to find a new way to classify all indirect goods and services, but rather to find a way how to cluster indirect items into groups (types of procurement) with similar procurement processes and requirements. In order to do so, the following steps are necessary:

1. Identify criteria that allow the characterization of indirect goods and services (see section 2.2.1).

2. Characterize items according to these criteria and set up a matrix where the characterization is done for some exemplary items (see section 2.2.2).

3. Cluster indirect goods and services into different procurement types according to their characteristics (see section 2.2.3).

2.2.1 Criteria to characterize indirect goods and services

The following sections provide a number of criteria that can be used to characterize indirect goods and services. They were chosen after screening available purchasing literature and after several interviews with experienced purchasing personnel.

2.2.1.1 Tangibility

Using the tangibility criteria to characterize items, a distinction has to be made between tangible and non-tangible items [Kotl1997, p. 433; Färb1998, p. 20]:

- *Tangible items* are "hard goods" or "physical goods".

- *Non-tangible* items include services, travel and entertainment, and any type of information ("soft") goods. Unlike "hard goods" they cannot be seen, tasted, felt, heard, or smelled before they are bought.

It is important to distinguish between tangible and intangible items, because the requirements for the purchasing process vary widely among those two groups. Purchasing physical items is very different from purchasing intangible items like services. The settlement process for services, for example, is very different from the settlement process for purchasing physical goods. In addition to that, the reception of a service is not a single event as it is with physical goods and the control of quality and completeness of delivery is more difficult. Besides the differences during the settlement phase, a purchase contract for services is usually more complex than a conventional purchase order. Since many services are unstructured and not standardized, the development and documentation of the requirements and specifications often involve more effort than the requisitioning of other indirect products.

Figure 7 shows how the tangibility criterion is used to differentiate within indirect goods and services.

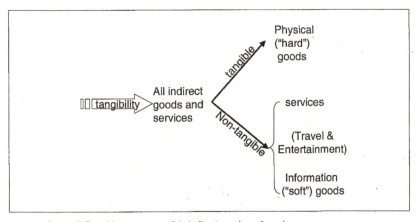

Figure 7: Tangible vs. non-tangible indirect goods and services

2.2.1.2 Accounting Rules

Purchases can be distinguished by the type of account they are charged to. Three different types of accounts can be differentiated [Färb1998, p. 19]:

- Inventory accounts,

- Asset accounts, and

- Expense accounts.

Direct or production material, which make up the direct procurement, are charged to *inventory accounts* and are part of the company's current assets, before they are converted during the production process [Houg92, p. 298-303; Dobl96, p.519].

Indirect goods and services are not necessarily appearing in the company's balance sheet. Items of high value are usually charged to *asset accounts* and depreciated over time. Thus, purchases in this category increase the companies fixed assets. Items of low value or non-durable goods such as services are mostly charged to *an expense account* within the month they are purchased. Consequently, these purchases reduce the profits of the company directly and don't appear in the company's balance sheet [Färb1998, p. 19].

2.2.1.3 Product complexity

Many products purchased by a company are not off-the-shelf products, but are either customized or have to be configured. In the manufacturing industry, for example, production equipment is usually more complex than any kind of office supplies. In the following a differentiation into low, medium and high complexity products is made:

- *Low complexity products* do not require the buyer to provide any kind of specifications. A product can usually be identified by an item number or a simple description and has a high level of standardization. Additionally, the same item can be bought from multiple suppliers by using the price as the only selection criteria. Therefore the procurement process is usually less complex. Office supplies and most MRO- (maintenance, repair, and operation) items fall into this category.

- Some products, as for example PCs, are modifiable to some extent according to the preferences of the buyer. These configurable products can in most cases be built from standardized components and are considered as of *medium complexity*.

- *High complexity* products, which often require the most complex procurement processes, are customized products. They are designed and built individually for a customer to fit its needs. In this case, the buyer has to select a supplier in advance. The relationship to a supplier of customized products is usually closer than to other suppliers.

The procurement of low complexity products and services is normally the easiest to automate. Therefore, functionality for purchasing low complex products and services is usually the easiest to implement in electronic commerce applications. Configurable products can still be specified without much effort, but require a certain type of configuration tool in order to be implemented in electronic commerce solution. Since customized products require extensive specifications they are less suitable for automation.

The following figure shows the relationship between the potential of automation and the complexity of a product or service. Note however that this is only a rough indicator for the automation potential of items and that each company has to evaluate separately if and how procurement automation for a certain item is possible.

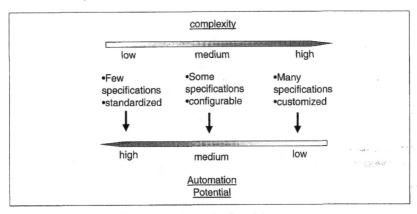

Figure 8: Product Complexity vs. Automation Potential

2.2.1.4 Transaction frequency

Not all indirect products and services are purchased with the same transaction frequency. Some need to be purchased on a daily basis, others are purchased just once. The frequency of transaction may determine the potential to automate a process, the type of contract that is in place with suppliers, the preferred payment method and other purchasing related variables. A differentiation between low, medium and high frequency is therefore presented:

- *Low frequency* transactions are considered nonrecurring or to occur only very few times. Purchases of consulting services or special machinery are examples for low frequency goods.

- Transactions that are done repeatedly but not on a daily basis will be considered as of *medium frequency.*

- *High frequency* transactions are those that occur repeatedly on a daily basis. The purchase of office supplies, for example, belongs to this category.

High frequency of transaction is an indicator of high potential for procurement process automation, because it justifies the set up cost for a procurement system supporting the purchasing processes. In contrary, low frequency of transaction usually indicates low potential for procurement process automation. The following figure depicts this correlation.

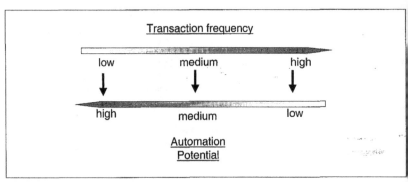

Figure 9: Transaction frequency vs. automation potential

2.2.1.5 Risk

Risk has many meanings and there is no simple definition. For some it indicates danger, for others harm or damage. From a management perspective, risk is generally considered as antithesis of benefit, thus a negative and undesirable factor [Gros1987, p. 24]. In this thesis the term risk will be used to express the danger or harm that a purchased item may have on the performance or operation of a company. If an item is needed and cannot be supplied in time or with the required quality it can have different risk involved depending on the items significance for company. Three levels of risk are going to be taken into consideration:

- *Low risk* items are those which do not affect the operation of a company in a direct way. They can also be considered as non-critical or non-strategic purchases. Usually the procurement of office supplies will be considered as of low risk because they normally don't represent any danger to company's performance and operation.

- *Medium risk* items do affect the performance but are not considered to be of strategic importance.

- *High risk* items have impact on the core business. In case they can't be supplied the company's operation is in danger. They can also be considered as being strategic or critical. Most of the direct procurement can be considered as being strategic, but also low value indirect procurement can sometimes be critical to the core business.

The risk criteria may impact the type of supplier relationship that is in place as well as the approval process.

2.2.1.6 Value

The criteria of value will be used as another variable to characterize purchased items. Value in this case will be understood as the actual price paid for an item, and not the individual perception. The value of a purchased item has impact on the procurement process especially regarding the buying technique used, the necessary approval process and the selected payment method.

There is no right or wrong way to determine weather an item should be considered as being of low, medium or high value. This will depend upon each company's policies and rules. Usually a differentiation will be done regarding the $-price of an item. Exemplary the following three categories are introduced, with variables A and B being the lower and upper bound of the categories:

- Low value items:< $ A

- Medium value: $ A < x < $ B

- High value: > $ B

Usually low to medium value items are charged directly to an expense account, where as high value items are charge to an asset account and depreciated over time.

Since the cost of processing a purchase order is estimated between $25 and $250, regardless of the value of the items being purchased [Dobl1996, p. 79], low value items originate relatively high transaction costs compared to the acquisition cost of the item. This problem is referred to in purchasing literature as small order problem [Dobl1984, p. 508].

Therefore significant savings can be obtained when simplifying and automating the procurement process of low value items. This is especially true, when in addition to that these items are purchase with a high transaction frequency. The focus in this case should be on transaction cost reduction.

On the other hand, for high value items that are purchased with a low transaction frequency, much bigger savings can be obtained by making the right purchase decision and lower the acquisition price of the item, instead of lowering the transaction costs.

The correlation is visualized in Figure 10. It is critical to understand the implications of this correlation, because it impacts to a great extend the type of procurement support that needs to be provided according to the characteristics of the items.

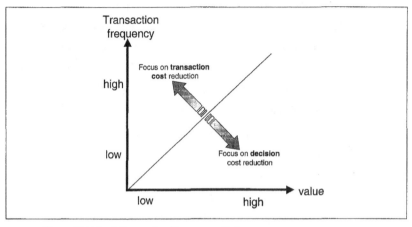

Figure 10: Value & Transaction Frequency criteria

2.2.1.7 Substitutability

Substitutability has to do with how easy an item can be replaced by another item of a different brand or make. Usually it comes along with product complexity, the level of standardization and how much an item differs among suppliers.

- *Low substitutability* means that it is hard to find an alternative item that will accomplish the same function. Usually each supplier has unique specifications.

- If items can be used interchangeable and there are very few differences among supplier, *high substitutability* is given.

The substitutability criteria has an impact on the type of supplier relation in place. Usually low substitutability means that a closer relation with suppliers is aspired, because switching among suppliers is more difficult. High substitutability, on the other hand, allows to switch among supplier easily.

2.2.2 Characterize indirect goods and services

The previous section introduced several criteria that can be used to characterize indirect goods and services. This section presents a matrix that allows the characterization of indirect goods and services according to the criteria depicted before. The criteria will be listed on the abscissa of the matrix whereas the ordinate will depict some exemplary goods and services.

Note however, that two important factors need to be taken into consideration when applying these criteria to characterize indirect goods and services:

1) Some of the above mentioned criteria can only be applied on a subset of items, and therefore do not hold for the entire range of indirect goods and services.

2) Some criteria can vary significantly from organization to organization. Criteria such as *risk* and *value* will perhaps depend more on the industry & individual company than on the item itself. For example, although printed materials would generally be considered a non-strategic, low value, and low risk item for most companies, they could very well be strategic goods for banks and other financial institutions.

	tangability	accounting	complexity	frequency	risk	value	substituability
pencil	tangible	expense	low	high	low	low	high
staple	tangible	expense	low	high	low	low	high
mouse	tangible	expense	low	medium	low	low	high
First Aid Kid	tangible	expense	medium	low	low	low	medium
Cleaning Supplies	tangible	expense	low	high	low	low	high
laptop	tangible	expense	medium	medium	medium	medium	medium
server	tangible	asset	high	low	high	high	low
car	tangible	asset	medium	medium	medium	high	high
ms-office	non tangible	expense	low	high	low	low	low
customized Software	non tangible	exp./ ass.	high	low	high	high	low
janitorial services	non tangible	expense	low	high	low	low	high
security services	non tangible	expense	low	high	low	low	high
consulting service	non tangible	exp./ ass.	high	low	high	high	low
oil-tubes	tangible	asset	medium	medium	medium	medium	medium
MRO	tangible	expense	low	high	low	low	high

Figure 11: Exemplary characterization of indirect goods and services

2.2.3 Clustering indirect goods and services

After having characterized some exemplary goods and services in the previous section, the next step is to cluster items with similar characteristics. The goal is to find groups of items, which have similar requirements regarding the procurement process as well as identical persons involved in the purchase decision of an item.

It should be taken into account that not all criteria apply to the entire range of indirect items and that some criteria may vary based on the industry & individual company (see previous section) when clustering into different types of procurement.

Since the tangibility criteria covers the entire range of indirect goods and services and does not vary regardless of industry & individual company, it seems suitable to be used in the first place to identify different procurement types on the highest level.

The tangibility criterion distinguished between physical goods, services, information goods and travel & entertainment (see section 2.2.1.1). This thesis will focus mainly on physical goods, and services. Travel & entertainment is not going to be discussed any further in this thesis and information goods are only analyzed in the context of the procurement of software.

Due to the increasing importance of Information technology, which has established itself as a vital strategic tool throughout industries and is undoubtedly becoming a more prominent feature of the business landscape, IT-procurement (hardware and software) will be analyzed in addition to the above depict groups.

IT procurement includes physical goods or tangible items (hardware: i.e. computer parts) and intangible items like information goods (software) and service. Resulting the three procurement types that are going to be analyzed more in detail throughout this thesis are:

1. Physical goods
2. Services

3. IT-Procurement

The differentiation into these three high level types of procurement it not enough, because within these groups the requirements and specifications still vary widely. For example: Specifying computer parts is different from office supplies and both are different from vehicle parts, even though they all belong to the procurement type of physical goods. On the side of services, engineering, financial, construction, legal, janitorial, clerical, and maintenance services have all different requirements and specifications.

There is no purchasing process that is suitable to supports these different types of procurement. Therefore, besides the tangibility criteria, other criteria depict in section 2.2.1 will be used to find procurement-types with similar requirements and specifications regarding the purchasing process. To do so, each of the above-identified high level procurement-types will be looked at more in detail.

2.2.3.1 Physical goods

There are several ways to distinguish between physical goods. The idea here is to define certain criteria that will make up a special group with the same requirements and specifications regarding the purchasing process. Two sub-types of procurement with almost diametrically opposed criteria characteristics are therefore going to be distinguished (note that not every physical good can be assigned to one of these two groups):

b) **Commodities**, defined in this thesis as tangible items of low value, low risk, high transaction frequency, high substitutability, low product complexity and charged to an expense account within a month they are purchased. Items that fall into this category include most office supplies (pencils, paper clips, scratch pads, erasers, staples and disks) as well as most MRO- (maintenance, repair, and operations) items. For these items it is virtually indistinguishable from which supplier they are bought and a special focus should be on lowering the transaction costs when purchasing these items.

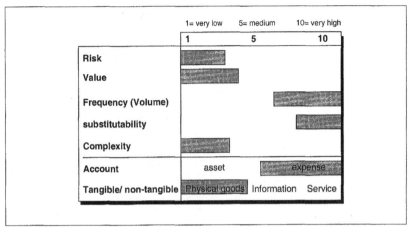

	1= very low	5= medium	10= very high
	1	5	10
Risk			
Value			
Frequency (Volume)			
substitutability			
Complexity			
Account	asset		expense
Tangible/ non-tangible	Physical goods	Information	Service

Figure 12: Profile for commodities

b) Capital equipment, defined as tangible items of relative high value that are usually purchased in low volume (low transaction frequency). In contrast to commodities, these items are charged to an asset account and are depreciated over time. Purchasing of capital equipment is usually complicated by the fact that products differ among suppliers. Each supplier normally has its own specification and each product may have slightly different characteristics to perform the same function [Houg1002, pp. 301-303]. Other characteristics are medium/high risk, medium/low substitutability and high product complexity. When purchasing capital equipment the focus should be more on lowering the decision making cost, than on lowering transaction costs (see 2.2.1.6).

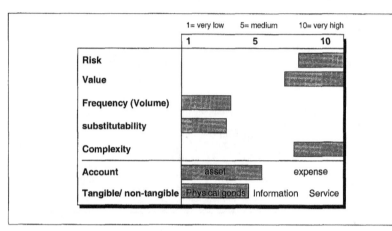

	1	5	10
Risk			▓▓▓
Value			▓▓▓
Frequency (Volume)	▓▓▓		
substitutability	▓▓▓		
Complexity			▓▓▓
Account	asset		expense
Tangible/ non-tangible	Physical goods	Information	Service

1= very low   5= medium   10= very high

Figure 13: Profile for Capital Equipment

2.2.3.2 Services

A service can be defined as "any act or performance that one party can offer to another that is essentially intangible and does not result in the ownership of anything." Its production may or may not be tied to a physical product. When the service is not tied to a physical product it is called pure service [Kotl1997, p. 467].

Two sub-types of service procurement are going to be distinguished, which are routine services and complex services. These two extremes, however, do not cover the entire range of services. It just defines two types of services that fulfill certain (diametrically opposed) criteria peculiarities.

a) Routine services are characterized as low value, low risk, high transaction frequency, low complexity (Statement of work (SOW) is low) and highly substitutable services that are charged to an expense account. Purchases of repair services, such as repair of computer hardware, office machines, plant equipment, automobiles and trucks, motors, and maintenance of fire extinguishers and flower services, janitorial service, park service, and catering fall into this category [Houg1992, p. 303].

28

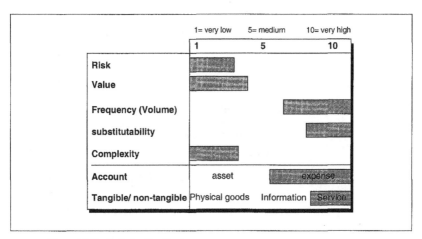

	1= very low	5= medium	10= very high
	1	5	10
Risk	▓▓		
Value	▓▓▓		
Frequency (Volume)			▓▓▓
substitutability			▓▓
Complexity	▓▓▓		
Account	asset		▓▓ expense
Tangible/ non-tangible	Physical goods	Information	▓ Service

Figure 14: Profile for routine Services

The profile of routine services suggests that there are similarities with the purchase of commodities.

b) Complex services are characterized as high value, high risk, low transaction frequency, high complexity (extensive Statement of Work) and low substitutable services. Consulting and outsourcing services fall into this category. Unlike routine services, standard specifications are unavailable for this type of service, thus, a unique, enforceable Statement Of Work (S.O.W.) must be developed [Burt1984, p..52]. The clarity, accuracy, and completeness of the S.O.W. is critical for the successful procurement of complex services [Dobl1996, pp. 410-411].

29

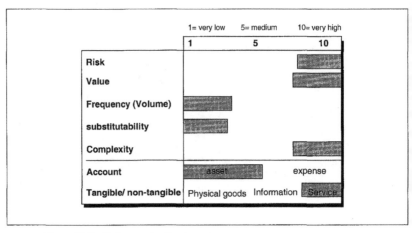

	1= very low	5= medium	10= very high
	1	**5**	**10**
Risk			▓▓▓
Value			▓▓
Frequency (Volume)	▓▓		
substitutability	▓▓		
Complexity			▓▓▓
Account	asset		expense
Tangible/ non-tangible	Physical goods	Information	Service

Figure 15: Profile for complex Services

2.2.3.3 IT Procurement

IT-Procurement in this thesis is defined as the purchasing of hardware and software. Hardware and software are inexorably linked and neither one is of much value without the other. They are only valuable because they work together as a system [Shap1999, pp. 2-3].

Since hardware is a tangible item and software an intangible item the requirement for the purchasing process differ widely (see section 2.2.1.1). Therefore both are going to be analyzed separately throughout this thesis.

a) **Hardware**: Hardware is the physical aspect of computers, telecommunications, and other information technology devices. The term "hardware" distinguishes the "box" and the electronic circuitry and components of a computer from the program (software) that runs on it. Hardware includes not only the computer proper but also the cables, connectors, power supply units, and peripheral devices such as the keyboard, mouse, audio speakers, and printers.

b) **Software**: Software is the instruction executed by a computer, as opposed to the physical device on which they run (the "hardware"). Software can be split into two main types:

- **Standard software** (like Ms Office) can be bought and installed off the shelf and therefore does not need any type of customization. Usually this type of software is of low value, low risk, high transaction frequency, high substitutability and low complexity. Standard software is normally charged to an expense account the month that it is purchased.

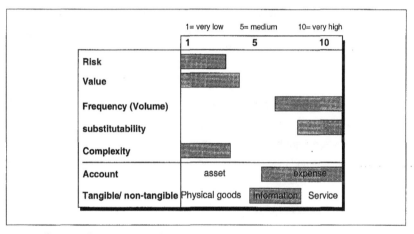

Figure 16: Profile for standard software

- **Customized software** (like ERP and Electronic Commerce Applications) usually can't be implemented off the shelf, but require significant customization in order to be implemented and used. This type of software normally is involved with high risk, high value, low transaction frequency, low substitutability and high complexity. Unlike standard software, customized software must be considered as a capital good that is charged to an asset account and is depreciated over time.

31

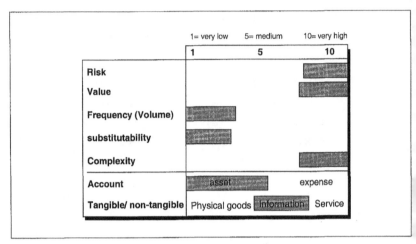

Figure 17: Profile for customized software

Now that different procurement types have been identified, it is important to analyze the specifics of each procurement type more in detail in the next step. The goal in the following chapter is to depict the "traditional" procurement process and to identify the special requirements of each type of procurement.

3 Analysis of different procurement types

In this section some of the above depict procurement types are addressed more in detail. The main purpose is to show the current or "traditional" purchasing process and identify the special user-requirements for each type of procurement. First, the procurement type of commodities will be analyzed more in detail in section 3.1. Next, the procurement of services (see section 3.2) and finally the procurement of Information Technology (see section 3.3) will be outlined.

3.1 Commodities

The intention of this section is to demonstrate how procurement of commodities is currently done and to show the problems occurring from the procurement process.

After a short characterization of commodities (see section 3.1.1), the people and their activities involved in the purchasing process will be introduced in section 3.1.2. Furthermore the purchasing process will be analyzed step by step more in detail (see section 3.1.3), and problems as well as resulting user requirements of each step of the procurement process will be depict.

3.1.1 Product Characterization

Commodities in this thesis were defined in section 2.2.3.1 as tangible items of low value, low risk, high transaction frequency, high substitutability, and low product complexity, which are charged to an expense account within the month they are purchased. Items that fall into this category include most office supplies (such as pencils, paper, paper clips scratch pads and staples) and most MRO (maintenance repair and operation) items.

An analysis of the items a buyer typically purchases shows, that approximately 80% of an organization's purchase orders are for these kind of items that constitute only for 20% of the purchased value [Fear1993, p. 650; Zenz1994, p. 55].

33

Furthermore, many organizations have followed the practice of turning each requisition for office and industrial supplies into a purchase order leading to many low-value transactions. Purchase orders usually cost between $25 and $250 to be processed, whether they are for items that cost $1000 or less than $100, not taking into account the requisition costs, receiving costs, or the invoice payment costs [Dobl1996, p. 79]. The procurement process of commodities is therefore characterized by the fact that the cost of processing a purchase order is usually higher than the value of the item itself.

Furthermore, since the items are standardized, technical specifications are equal throughout the market and the brands. Therefore, the source of supply is a less important factor than the price of the item (multiple suppliers may be addressed to purchase the item).

Unique about purchasing commodities is that the request develops decentralized across the company at every end-user desk. That is the reason why, although there is a high volume request, the items are often purchased in small numbers and it is difficult to pool purchases across an organization in order to negotiate better conditions.

Now, that the first overview of the procurement of commodities has been depict, the persons involved in the procurement process and their activities are going to be introduced.

3.1.2 Persons involved in the purchasing process

Most likely there are three different participants taking part in the purchasing process of buying commodities. They are:

- The **end-user** who defines the need and requests an item (see section 3.1.2.1)

- the **purchasing department** who works on the requests, which they receive from the end-user (see section 3.1.2.2), and

- the **budget holder** who authorizes and funds the purchase (see section 3.1.2.3).

The involvement of each of these participants in the procurement process is going to be explained in the following sections.

3.1.2.1 End-user

The end-user is the one who usually develops the need. He may be spread out across the whole company and his request may only be centralized in the purchasing department where all the orders will be gathered. Usually the end-user has no knowledge about purchasing and is more concerned about quality, functionality and fast delivery than price or source of supply.

The end-user starts the purchasing process on the operational level (see section 3.1.2.2) with the definition of need. He then turns the responsibility into the hands of the purchasing personnel by sending out the purchase requisition with the description of need. From this point on, the purchasing department deals with buying the requested items.

3.1.2.2 Purchasing department

The purchasing department are the buying professionals of an organization and are involved on two different levels of procurement. On the strategic level they are involved in all activities that are usually completed before or after the actual purchase. On the operational level they are involved in the actual purchase of the items.

On the **strategic level**, the purchasing department is involved in information and sourcing (finding new or better suppliers), in negotiation (negotiating prices, quality, terms of delivery, etc. with their suppliers), in contracting (setting up the contracts that will be used by the purchasing department), and implementation. Other purchasing activities on the strategic level include the measurement and evaluation of supplier performance as well as identifying buying patterns and habits of end-users.

On the **operational level** the purchasing department works for and together with the end-users. Once the end-user stated his request it is the purchasing department who does the actual buying. They write the request and start the approval process, manage the delivery and payment procedures and provide order tracking information for the end user.

The purchasing department currently spends most of its time on the operational level. According to a recent study of the *Purchasing Magazine,* operating and administration activities represent 80 percent of the time, effort and cost of a typical procurement department, while only 20% of the activities are spend for strategic activities. However, these 20%, which are devoted to strategic development and supplier relations generate the more significant long-term results. They are actually the activities that are value-adding while the activities on the operational level add little or no value at all [Port1993, p. 41].

3.1.2.3 Budget Holder

The budget holder is involved on the strategic level of purchasing setting the long term goals for the purchasing department. On the operational level they are responsible for authorizing (approving) and funding the purchase request in case that the value of the purchased item exceeds a certain value. Usually however, there is no approval necessary in the case of buying commodities.

3.1.3 Purchasing process

Many large companies have adopted such applications as enterprise resource planning (ERP), advanced planning and scheduling (APS) or material requirements planning (MRP) software to replenish production supplies automatically. However, they still use paper requisition forms to purchase non-production supplies. If an employee needs a commodity, he or she typically

- fills out a paper form for the purchase requisition and the description of need,

- sends the requisition through inter-office mail to a company buyer,

- and waits for the purchasing personnel to approve the order and phone, fax or mail a purchase order to the supplier [Shap1998, pp. 32 – 35].

The manual procurement process consists of several steps that are necessary to process a request and order a product. It starts with the definition of need (information), gathering product information such as price, quality or functionality, sourcing the right supplier and writing the requisition.

An approval process will be started in case the values of the requested items exceed a certain limit. Once the request is approved and intern stocks are checked for non-availability of the requested items the purchasing personnel will send out a purchase order. The moment the products are delivered and the inspection of incoming items is finished payment will be executed. In the case of commodities an after sales support will most likely not be necessary.

For each step during the procurement process a transaction of information is necessary and therefore responsible for the time and cost consuming process. Information can be processed by phone, fax, email, walking paper, or verbal order among others.

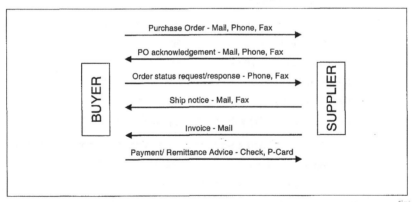

Figure 18: Buyer-Supplier information exchange (Source: Intraware Présentation, Dez.98)

Buyers and suppliers exchange information through different kinds of media. As seen in the above figure there are several transactions necessary to exchange all information. These processes are time intensive and costly. Therefore it can take days or weeks for an employee to receive the ordered product. The process is very inefficient and therefore encourages maverick buying among employees, who can obtain products more quickly by ordering directly from convenient suppliers and then asking the company for reimbursement. The problem is, the supplier may not be among the company's preferred suppliers – those that offer volume discounts based on pre-negotiated contracts. Purchasing professionals refer to this problem as "contract leakage". It means companies are unable to aggregate purchase volume and leverage their non-production spending.

In the following the major steps of the procurement process for the purchase of commodities will be described more in detail and problems will be depict.

The procurement process for commodities is a workflow of the following basic steps: Definition of need (information), requisitioning, approval, purchase order, delivery, payment and after sales support.

3.1.3.1 Definition of need (information)

Before the first phase of a potential transaction the buyer develops and defines a need and evaluates information for the item that he wants to request. End-users can search in paper catalogs for the items they need. These catalogs are often outdated and do not provide the best offer on the market. In addition, the catalogs do not necessarily present the offers of those suppliers, which are currently contracted by the purchasing department.

Definitions of need arise from all end-users of all departments decentralized in an organization. Once they are defined and information is evaluated a description of the need must be written. This description is part of the requisition (see next section) that the end-user sends to the purchasing department.

3.1.3.2 Requisitioning

The purchase requisition is used to communicate the need of items within an organization, and contains information about specifics, such as:

- what does the end-user need (product information),
- who is requesting the items (end-user information), and
- where does the request come from.

Before purchasing is forwarding the purchase requisition for approval by an authorized manager, it is necessary to check if the need can be met from available store stock or if the need can be aggregated with any other outstanding similar requests [Cupg1998, p. 2]. The end-user requests need to be collected and aggregated by the centrally operating purchasing department to be able to buy from contracted suppliers and receive volume discounts.

3.1.3.3 Approval

Participants in the approval process are the end-user (waiting for the purchase requisition to be approved), the purchasing personnel (trying to proceed the approval) and the authorized approver (in case of commodities sometimes equal to the purchasing personnel).

After the purchasing department has received the requisition, they forward the end-user request to the authorized person. The end-user, waiting for the request to be approved, usually receives no information about the approval status. Therefore, end-users request information from the purchasing personnel. This is time consuming for the end-user as well as the purchasing personnel. Consequently, especially the purchasing personnel has less time to concentrate on more important strategic activities (refer to section 3.1.2.2).

Once the purchase requisition is approved, purchasing personnel submits the purchase order.

3.1.3.4 Purchase order

The purchase order expresses the agreement between the buyer and the supplier. Once accepted by the supplier, it has the legal force of a binding contract. Therefore, companies demand written acceptance of the order from the supplier, which is called the acknowledgment order. Usually three different types of purchase orders are necessary:

- The original purchase order (sent to the vendor),

- the acknowledgment order , and

- an order for the purchasing department.

Copies may also go to the receiving department (location of the end-user), accounting, quality control, and the requisitioner (end-user) [Hein1991, pp. 74-75]. This process is time consuming because purchase orders must not only be written and processed but also entered in a data system to match order payment and delivery. Furthermore, many paper forms must be transferred between different departments and persons, which needs additional time.

Once the order has been submitted the responsibilities of the purchasing department do not end. Orders need to be followed (order tracking) to ensure that the seller has received the order and that delivery occurs as requested [Zens1994, p.12]. In addition, the order tracking information must also be forwarded to the requesting end-user.

3.1.3.5 Delivery

The function of the receiving department (which can either be an adjunct of the purchasing or the stores department) is to receive incoming goods and sign the delivery notice presented by the carrier or the supplier in connection with the shipment. Receiving activity time includes quantity and price correction, reversals and claims [Hein1991, p. 77].

After the supplier has delivered the required items, the delivery has to be forwarded to the end-user (requester). Once the items reached their destination, purchasing receives an invoice that has to be inspected for correctness before payment is initiated [Faer1998, p. 33].

3.1.3.6 Payment

Several payment mechanisms can be used (e.g. check payment or electronic funds transfer), depending on the relationship to the particular buyer to balance the invoice. Overall, payment is time consuming because invoices need to be processed, which includes receiving, filing and scanning, distributing and data entry. Therefore, organizations have introduced flexible payment procedures to reduce and simplify the payment activities. Among those are: Petty Cash System, Cash on Delivery and Purchasing Cards.

Once the delivered items are received, the invoice has been inspected and payment is transferred, the order can be closed.

3.1.3.7 After Sales Support

In the case of commodities, after sales support will not be of importance due to the items' characteristic depict in chapter 2.2.3.1.

3.1.4 Conclusion

As shown in the previous analyzed procurement process (section 3.1.3) there are problems in every steps of the process. End-users have to search in outdated catalogs and spend time by describing their needs and sending purchase requisitions. Purchasing personnel is busy answering end-user requests about approval status and order tracking. Information needs to be duplicated on multiple paper forms and distributed to several departments and persons. In addition, the paper forms must not only be filed but also entered in the data system. Overall, the procurement process needs too much time because too many people are involved in the procurement process and too much information must be transferred by paper, phone or fax.

End-users are frustrated of the inefficient and time consuming procurement process. Therefore, they start to purchase off-contract to avoid slow procedures.

This problem is referred to as contract leakage or maverick buying. End-users circumventing the procurement process are limiting the ability for purchasing to buy from preferred suppliers and receive negotiated contract prices. Furthermore, purchasing is not able to collect detailed data of buying habits and create spending patterns. Consequently, they weaken a company's buying power.

To solve these problems the procurement process needs to be simplified, and automated as much as possible. In addition, purchasing personnel needs to reduce their involvement in the operational process and concentrate more on value-adding activities. The objective is to put contracted vendors at the end-user fingertips with up-to-date product description and pricing as well as to automate the purchasing process as much as possible. The goal is to make the process from describing the need to delivery and payment, paperless. In addition, have maximum control of end-user spending and loose no information regarding end-user spending patterns. Consequently, the main result from automating and streamlining the purchasing process of commodities is to reduce time and therefore lower transaction costs.

To reach these goals the procurement process needs to be automated by implementing a flexible procurement system. Resulting from the problems analyzed above this system needs to fulfill certain requirements.

- The system needs to provide a user-friendly front end, which can be operated by occasional and non-professional end-users.

- Electronic catalogs with up to date content and pricing that are easy and fast to search.

- Powerful search engines within the electronic catalogs.

- Flexible approval routing and the possibility of constant approval order updating for the requester.

- Integration with existing data systems to provide information within the whole organization.

- Order tracking functions to keep track of the delivery schedule.

- Payment support for fast and secure money transfer.

How Internet based technologies and systems will affect the procurement process and are able to fulfill the user requirements will be analyzed in section 5.1.

3.2 Purchasing Services

The procurement of services is a little-understood, but increasingly important, activity [Burt1990, p. 108]. Expenditures on services by commercial firms, governments and not-profit organizations in some cases represent more than 25 percent of the organization's expenditures. In many cases the impact of the services themselves on the success of the organization's operation is far greater than the impact of the dollar spent. Often they are of critical importance to the operation of the organization [Dobl1996, p. 408-409].

Obtaining services is one of purchasing's most challenging responsibilities. In no other area is there a more complex interdependency between the purchase description (statement of work), method of compensation, source selection, contract administration, and satisfied customer [Burt1990, p. 91 –108; Dobl1996, p. 409].

In 2.2.3.2, service was defined as "any act or performance that one party can offer to another that is essentially intangible and does not result in the ownership of anything."

Buying services is therefore very different from buying products. Purchasing services, unlike the acquisition of materials, supplies, or equipment, demands greater knowledge of the generally labor intensive supplier base, as well as the competitive posture of the buying organization. Often, the policies and procedures that guide the procurement of manufactured goods will not help in the selection of the best supplier and subsequent administration and evaluation of a service contract. Yet, too often, the same company acts as though they were buying a commodity rather than a service [Fear1993, pp. 698-706]. One of the main differences derives from the way in which tangible goods and intangible services can be specified. The **specification** for a copy machine (a tangible good), for example, can be both tangible and specific, containing requirement like:

- Single side copy and a throughput of a least 20 pages per minute
- Capacity to assemble, collate, and staple documents of at least 50 sheets
- Enlargement/reduction ratios of from 3/1 to 1/8
- Mean time before failure of at least 1000 hours.

Using the same model and procedure to obtain a service, the following specifications might be prepared:

- Up to 160 person-hours
- Up to 150 manuscript pages
- Delivery of manuscript within four month

Each of these specifications are tangible and measurable. Yet they don't specify the actual need that has to be addressed. The service offers obtained with these specifications are most likely going to be quite different and most certainly not going to achieve the primary objective. Therefore special procedures that guide the procurement of services are necessary and explained in the following sections.

3.2.1 Routine and complex services

Not all services are purchased the same way. Some services can be purchased using the same techniques applicable to the purchasing of commodities; other services require additional unique considerations.

In section 2.2.3.2 a differentiation into routine and complex services was presented. **Routine services** are characterized as being of low value, low risk, high transaction frequency, low complexity (Statement of work (SOW) is low) and highly substitutable. Purchases for repair services, such as repair of computer hardware, other office machines, plant equipment, automobiles and trucks, motors, and maintenance of fire extinguishers, to mention the most common and flower services, janitorial service, park service, catering and accounting services fall into this category. For this type of services, clear and precise specifications can easily be prepared. These services can be purchased utilizing the same techniques used to buy commodities (refer to section 3.1) and are therefore not analyzed more in detail in this section [Dobl1984, pp. 193-194].

The focus of this section is on the procurement of **complex services**, such as consulting services, which involve the use of a wide variety of unique considerations [Dobl1984, pp. 193-194]. Standard specifications are unavailable for this type of service, thus, a unique, enforceable Statement Of Work (S.O.W.) must be developed [Burt1984, p.52]. The clarity, accuracy, and completeness of the S.O.W is critical for the successful service procurement [Dobl1996, pp. 410-411].

3.2.2 Persons involved in the purchasing process

Purchasing's involvement in the procurement of complex services is different than in the procurement of commodities. While in the procurement of commodities three different participants, with different activities, tasks and responsibilities could be identified (refer to section **Fehler! Verweisquelle konnte nicht gefunden werden.**), the procurement of complex services is usually done in a **team**. Joint planning session are organized where the buyer and representatives from all interested functions, such as the requesting, legal, finance and quality assurance department, define and formulate the Statement Of Work. In many instances it is even advisable to invite pre-qualified potential suppliers to help develop the S.O.W. and enhance the customer's ultimate satisfaction. Usually participation by top, middle, and lower level management personnel is required during the procurement process [Burt1990, p. 95, Fear1993, p. 701].

45

Not always however purchasing participates in these sessions. In many service areas purchasing is often not involved, and service contractors frequently work very hard to keep purchasing out. By avoiding and bypassing purchasing's involvement in the procurement of services, contractors (suppliers) avoid:

- Written specifications

- Any detailed analysis of costs

- Breaking down billing charges and requirements for receipts, and

- Negotiating.

Managers who buy without purchasing assistance often are seen as easy marks by sellers, because they are usually to busy to negotiate patiently and get into details, and in addition to that, have no knowledge of the current market [Burt1990, pp. 91-93].

3.2.3 Purchasing cycle

The definition of a need or requirement by the end-user is the first step towards the purchase of a service and initiates the purchasing cycle. If, after consideration of all relevant factors, the decision is made to purchase the service from a service supplier, the requestor usually creates a purchase requisition. Following receipt of the request, the buyer's responsibility is to oversee the development of a statement of work (SOW). Usually a joint planning session will be organized where the buyer and representatives from all interested functions refine the definition of the requirement, and an assignment is made for one or more of the individuals to write an SOW for the undertaking [Fear1993, pp. 698-708].

The entire procurement process for purchasing complex services is a sequence or workflow consisting of several steps that are depict in Figure 19. The process begins with the definition of need, and ends with the pre-award conference.

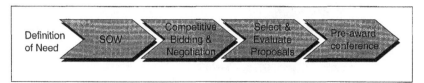

Figure 19: Purchasing cycle for the procurement of services

In the following each steps of the procurement process will be analyzed more in detail.

3.2.3.1 Statement of work

The most critical ingredient to a successful procurement of services is the development and documentation of the requirements – the statement of work (S.O.W.). One of the objectives of writing a statement of work is to gain understanding and an agreement with a contractor concerning the specific nature of the technical effort to be performed. The statement of work identifies what the contractor is to accomplish. The clarity, accuracy, and completeness of the S.O.W. determine, to a large degree, weather the objectives of the contract will be achieved. [Dobl1996, pp. 410-411].

The SOW is a description of the work to be performed. It should identify measurable or verifiable performance and acceptance criteria. Furthermore, the SOW should clearly explain how the service provider will be expected to adhere to any fiscal, schedule and performance criteria. The SOW asks for example: How the work will be accomplished from its initiation to termination, what materials (financial records internal and external) the supplier will need to complete the work and when these materials will be requested from the buyer. The buyer will then furnish a complete set of evaluation criteria for all proposals as well as performance criteria for acceptance of service delivery. After the statement of work has been developed the buyer usually explains the complete purchasing cycle, from the development of the SOW to postaward administration of the contract, to all involved individuals. The buyer then should confer with the appropriate individuals concerning the identification of qualified service providers that can satisfactorily complete the statement of work. Where necessary, the buyer may conduct market surveys, initiate networking activities for experience verification, and review published sources for identification of potential service suppliers [Fear1993, p. 704-706].

Usually two phases are necessary for the development and documentation of a clear, complete ,and accurate Statement of Work [Dobl1996, p. 411]:

- Planning the Statement of Work: The planning phase is aimed at a thorough investigation of the why and what of the project. The exact tasks and details that need to be included in the S.O.W. are determined in this phase.

- Writing the Statement of Work: The S.O.W. must maintain a delicate balance between protecting the buyer's interests and encouraging the supplier's (contractor) creativity during both proposal preparation and contract performance.

3.2.3.2 Competitive bidding and negotiation:

At this point of the process the buyer should decide whether to competitively bid or negotiate the purchase. Regardless of the method selected, the buyer should define clearly the nature and scope of the procurement (the SOW), the award criteria (price, service, quality, delivery time), the required delivery date, and the timing for the award decision [Fear1993, p. 706].

The choice between bidding and negotiation typically depends on (a) the nature of the competitive environment (b) the nature of the service (c) the continuity of service delivery [Fear1993, p. 706].

The buyer should also decide which buying vehicle to use – purchase order, a systems contract, or a service agreement. The vehicle selected will affect the service delivery by the successful provider through the expectations for the provider's adherence to it and the buyer's monitoring or performance criteria [Fear1993, p. 707].

3.2.3.3 Selecting service contractors – proposal evaluation

When purchasing services, selecting the "right" source is much more of an art than when purchasing physical goods. Based on the complexity of many service procurements and the unexpected problems, which tend to arise, it usually is desirable to choose established, reputable suppliers. Unless one supplier has a special skill or a unique reputation, selection of supplier should be based on a careful review of the competing firm [Burt1990, p. 99].

During source selection several questions should be taken into consideration [Fear1993, pp. 698-708]:

- Does the service firm understand the need?
- Is the proposed solution clear?
- Does the proposed solution meet the need?
- Is the service firm willing and able to deliver the solution when needed?
- Are the provisions for quality control?
- Are there adequate review milestones?

Furthermore, a buyer of services must evaluate both, the financial outlay and the opportunity cost, along with expected service quality and needs, when selecting from among the various types of potential suppliers.

Since services are by nature intangible, some value judgements inevitably must be made in assessing each supplier's proposal. The following analyses are sometimes employed:

1. *Cost analysis*: An examination of the cost for each component of the service as it impacts the quality and total price of the service.

2. *Value analysis*: An analysis of the nature and scope of the proposed service relative to the defined need and the cost.

3. *Life-cycle costing*: An analysis of the total cost of the service, including all operating and follow-on costs, throughout the life of the service being transformed.

4. *Learning-curve applications*: An analysis of the expected increase in productivity associated with continued service delivery, and its impact of the cost of performing the service.

5. *Project management techniques*: An analysis of post award administration activities through the use of Gantt charts, PERT/CPM systems, etc, to monitor and control service schedules, cost and quality.

The objective of the buying team is, to select the one that best fulfills the buying organization's statement of work and related requirements, providing the greatest expected value for the organization [Fear1993, pp. 698 – 709].

3.2.3.4 Pre-award conference:

After careful evaluation of all bids or the completion of negotiations, a pre-award conference with the successful supplier is held. In the case of most service procurements, the establishment and maintenance of a strong two-way communication is essential to sustaining the desire level of supplier performance. This conference serves to define all expectations of the procurement action, from post-award administration of performance to the mechanics of payment. The award is then made and the service delivery begins.

Post-award administration activities are an integral component to the procurement of services. Unlike the procurement of a tangible product, buying services entails managing the supplier in its execution of service delivery. It is an important aspect of the purchasing cycle because the conduct of service delivery affects the operation of the buying organization [Fear1993, pp. 701 –711].

3.2.4 Conclusion

In contrast with the acquisition of a product, the buying of services requires a greater appreciation for the effect that the delivery of various services can have on the attitudes and the productivity of the people involved. These, in turn, frequently translate into profit.

The development of a well-defined statement of work for a service procurement often is more difficult than the development of a material specification, simply because of the open-ended nature of most service activities and the difficulty in defining a specific work routine. Additionally, selection of a service provider necessitates knowledge of not only the firm, but also the individuals performing the work. Evaluation of a service proposal thus involves some independence on qualitative judgments along with quantitative assessments. Since a supplier's pricing strategy for delivery of services differ from those used for materials, a buyer's options for addressing these strategies require a comprehensive knowledge of various analytical tools identified with the analysis of price and cost.

In contrast to the purchase of commodities, where the focus is on driving costs out of the purchasing process by automating and simplifying the process, the focus when purchasing complex services should be in making the **"right"** purchasing **decisions**. Therefore, when looking for Internet based Technologies and Systems able to support this type of purchase, special attention should be given to this requirement.

3.3 IT-Procurement

Throughout industries the use of Information Technology (IT) has established itself as a vital strategic tool and is undoubtedly becoming a more prominent feature of the business landscape. When properly employed, the use of Information Technology allows organizations to support and generate business value by creating competitive advantage [Demp1997, pp. 81-91].

A sound IT-infrastructure always consists of hardware and software. Hardware and software are inexorably linked and neither one is of much value without the other. They are only valuable because they work together as a system [Shap1999, pp. 2-3].

In the past, it was fairly easy to figure out the cost of an IT-investment when considering to purchase new software and hardware. The cost for a new software application, for instance, was just the extra mainframe and disk capacity required, some developer time, and maybe some software licenses [Demp1997, p. 127].

Today, hardware and software may cost less, but hard-to-predict support and maintenance costs, business costs associated with the transition to a new system, and other hidden costs can more than double the initial investment. Additionally, information technology gets deeply integrated into most businesses, that it is almost impossible to be isolated as a variable [Demp1997, p. 127].

Therefore it is becoming increasingly difficult to determine the absolute value of information technology to an organization and make the right purchasing or investment decision. A selection based solely on cost, or even on the total cost of ownership may lead to bad decisions.

In the following a new approach called "total value of ownership" will be introduced briefly (see section 3.3.1), that might help to determine whether an IT-investment is worth while, by considering not only the hard facts, but also the "softer" more qualitative benefits of a purchase decision. Afterwards the persons who are usually involved in the procurement process of information technology will be introduced (see section 3.3.2). This section ends with a separate analysis of hardware (see section 3.3.3) and software (see section 3.3.4). For each some special requirements and considerations will be outlined.

3.3.1 Total value of ownership

The "total value of ownership" (TVO) is a new approach developed by Mckinsey & Company [Demp1998, pp. 127–137] that allows to evaluate the investment in Information Technology.

In contrast to low value, low risk items like commodities (see section 3.1), purchasing decisions regarding Information Technology can not be based just on the actual **acquisition cost** of an item. They need to take into consideration a variety of other costs associated with the ownership of an item, such as pre-acquisition costs, downtime costs, support and maintenance costs, and disposal costs. This approach is called **"total cost of ownership"** (TCO) and was designed to identify and measure components of expense beyond the initial cost of acquisition and implementation. It takes into account the cost projected over the entire life of an investment.

However, even this broader view also has limitations and is not a sound basis for decision making, because the TCO analysis often leaves out important cost categories such as complexity costs and they **ignore benefits** altogether, such as a gain in market share or an increase in customer loyalty. Payoffs like these are not controllable and depend on other business functions. Additionally, they also neglect soft and strategic factors, lack a well-defined base for comparison, and have difficulty evaluating lifecycle costs.

Applying the TCO when purchasing Information Technology can therefore lead to decisions such as replacing all PCs with cheaper dump terminals or switching vendors every month to get the lowest PC prices, because TCO focuses only on costs, but does not consider the benefits associated with the decision.

The "**total value of ownership**"-approach addresses this problem and considers purchasing decisions based on value. This means that in addition to the cost projected over the entire life of an investment also the "**softer**" more qualitative benefits of an investments are taken into account. The TVO-approach has three ingredients: a sound cost/ benefit methodology to evaluate the incremental value created by IT investments; robust management processes that integrate IT into normal business planning; and the maturity business judgment to make difficult tradeoffs effectively. For a more in depth analysis of this approach refer to [Demp1998, pp. 127-137].

The following figure gives an overview of the approaches presented above.

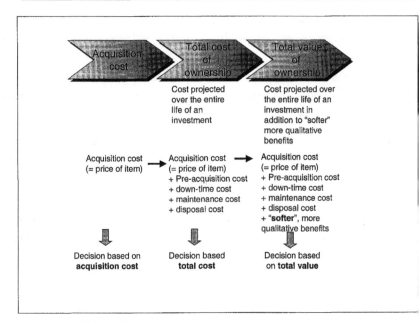

Figure 20: Total value of ownership

Now that an approach has been introduces that allows to evaluate IT decisions based on "hard"-, as well as "soft" facts, the persons involved in purchasing of IT will be presented.

3.3.2 Persons Involved

According to a recent survey by the Purchasing Magazine the procurement department is involved in 89% of the purchasing decisions regarding computers, networks (peripherals) and software. The extend of involvement includes activities like determining requirements, selecting suppliers, negotiating agreements and measuring supplier performance. According to 71% of the buyers asked the involvement in purchasing technology has grown during the past 3 years. 90% of the surveyed purchasers consider IT-procurement a **team effort** in which besides the purchasing personnel other departments are involved. The team for purchasing information technology therefore consists of representatives of the top management, the information technology department, the finance accounting personnel, and the end-users [Aver1998, Jun.18].

Their involvement in purchasing IT is as follows: The end-user determines what functionality is needed and the IT-department establishes the requirements and is responsible for technical specifications (standards and compatibility). They both know what they want but do not know how to get it cost-effectively. Purchasing on the other hand has the knowledge how to find new sources, how to negotiate conditions and how to set up contracts with suppliers. They therefore select the suppliers, make sure that company policies and financial objectives are met, negotiate the agreement, and manage the relationship. Finance in the end determines whether the purchase is justifiable.

Besides the end-user, the IT-department, and the purchasing department, it is critical to involve top management in IT decision, because of the strategic importance and long term impact that IT has on the overall performance of an organization.

In the following some specifics about the procurement of hardware and software will be introduced.

3.3.3 Procurement of Hardware

Hardware is the physical aspect of computers, telecommunications, and other information technology devices. In a broader sense it can be considered as the "Technology Infrastructure". The term "hardware" distinguishes the "box" and the electronic circuitry and components of a computers and related items from the program (software). Hardware includes not only the computer proper but also the cables, connectors, power supply units, and peripheral devices such as the keyboard, mouse, audio speakers, and printers.

Hardware implies permanence and invariability. It is, however possible to change the modular configurations that most computers come with by adding new adapters or cards that extend the computer's capabilities. Therefore, configuration, compatibility, and standards are key aspects that need to be considered when purchasing hardware.

3.3.3.1 Requirements and consideration of hardware purchasing

Before considering buying hardware, it is important to understand and consider the nature and special requirements of this type of product. The most important ones are listed in the following:

- Hardware purchasing decisions have to be based on the **"total value of ownership"** (see 3.3.1 Total value of ownership).

- Hardware must be considered a critical good because computer failure may cause a company to stop operate (high-risk good). Computers are the heart of most business processes and therefore must provide great **reliability and performance**.

- **Standardization** is a very important issue when purchasing hardware for a company. Not only for the reason of achieving high compatibility but also because standardizing computer equipment used throughout a company help to lower inventory levels, as well as costs of installation, support and training [Aver1998, Nov. 5]. Additionally, standardization leads to homogeneity and ease of interconnection between devices, which increases flexibility [Demp1997, p. 85].

- Due to the modularity and configuration ability of hardware, **compatibility** of different components becomes critical. Components need to be compatible with existing hardware devices and software applications need to be easy to integrate.

- Due to technology advances, **upgrades** on technology are introduced very frequently and need to be considered.

To ensure that these requirements are taken into account, organizations usually have **guidelines** in place to support purchasing decisions. These guidelines protect the company's investment by ensuring that the procurement department purchases high quality and appropriate products that have a reasonable live span. Furthermore they make purchasing easier by reducing the variety of items that need to be supported and make it possible to streamline the purchasing process.

3.3.4 Procurement of Software

Software is the instruction executed by a computer, as opposed to the physical device on which they run (the "hardware"). It is a general term for the various kinds of programs used to operate computers and related devices.

Software was split in section 2.2.3.3 into two main types, Standard software and Customized Software. In the following section some requirements of software purchasing are depict, which in most cases hold for both types of software.

While looking for information regarding the procurement of software, it is remarkable that almost the entire purchasing literature used in this thesis does not deal with this topic at all, even though today it is considered to be among the most critical and challenging purchases. Most of the information used in the following section is therefore based on recent articles and Internet-publications.

3.3.4.1 Requirements and considerations of software purchasing

To understand the procurement of software it is important to know that software is an asset that the corporation does not own. A software product is not a physical asset, but rather an expression of a set of ideas. Like a book, software is intellectual property. Domestic and international copyright laws protect software and, by extension, regulate its use. So, rather than simply purchasing a Software product, corporate buyers acquire **"rights to use"** software [Houg1992, p. 319].

The allowable scope of use of the product is defined in, and limited by, the terms and conditions contained in a **software license agreement** (SLA). Consequently, all of the terms and conditions found in agreements negotiated with software publishers or resellers become critical. If these needs or requirements are not properly defined, and/or if rights to use are not flexible, then the buying organization could end up paying for something that has little value to it.

Therefore corporate buyers need to ensure that they get the full value of their acquisition and see that the needs of their end users a met as the organization changes. Negotiating terms and conditions of an agreement become extremely important in software right to use. Since more leverage with suppliers usually means better terms and conditions for buyers, it is important to pool software purchases across a plant, division, or company and providing enough volume with which the company can negotiate lower prices with suppliers. However, since software gets integrated into the company's infrastructure, the corporate buyer loses some of that initial leverage. As a result, the buyer cannot easily terminate the relationship with an existing supplier and acquire the product from another supplier [Aver1998, Sep. 15; Feld1999]. This problem is referred to in literature as **"lock-in"** and is explained more in detail in [Shap1999, pp. 136-141].

There are several different ways buyers can compensate suppliers for rights to use software. Fees can be based on the number of users, the number of copies, etc. [Feld1999].

One possibility to purchase software is to have a license agreement with the software vendor. Under a license agreement, a corporate purchasing manager negotiates with a publisher for a specified number of licenses for software to be used by the company during a set period of time, typically 2-3 years. The publisher, in turn, sells the buyer the licenses at a discounted price, based on projected volume. This way, the buyer does not take delivery of a physical package; but acquires only the number of licenses, user manuals, and media to distribute the software that the company requires. For the buyer, the process of acquiring software licenses off an agreement dramatically reduces the number of transactions and the cost of processing them [Aver1997, Jan. 16].

Purchasing software can also be done with the help of a third person, a reseller. The value of a reseller lies in its expertise of licensing terms and conditions, and how they are applicable to a specific customer. The reseller also may negotiate directly with the publisher on behalf of a customer. For a smaller publisher not accustomed to filling volume orders, the reseller may supply the actual standardized form for the agreement. The reseller provides end-user training and support (including manuals), and helps purchasing with internal marketing efforts. Additionally the reseller can assist with implementing agreements at overseas sites, helping corporate buyers overcome such barriers as language difficulties and laws regarding intellectual property [Aver1997, Jan. 16].

Besides the critical importance that software license agreement play when purchasing software, there are some other characteristic of software that need to be taken into consideration before purchasing this type of good. Most of them were already mentioned with regards to purchasing hardware (see 3.3.3.1) and are therefore only cited in brief outlines:

- Total value of ownership

- Ease of use and performance

- Standards, compatibility, and frequent updates.

4 Internet based Technologies & Systems for indirect procurement

In Chapter 2 the fundamentals of procurement were outlined and different types of indirect procurement were identified. In Chapter 3 a detailed analysis of the identified procurement types was presented. For each of them the procurement process and the special requirements were outlined, depicting the **"traditional"** way of purchasing indirect goods and services.

With the commercialization of the Internet new ways to connect buyers, sellers, and intermediaries in Electronic Marketplaces have emerged and consequently new opportunities to support the exchange of goods and services, are possible. These Marketplaces can be set up for all different types of product categories, and are creating value by making trade between different market partners more efficient. According to an estimate of McKinsey & Company [Berr1998, p.152], which is based on case studies and interviews of players from a mix of industries, the experience of early participants suggests that an electronic marketplace can capture savings of 10 – 20 percent compared to the "traditional" marketplace. Therefore the potential value at stake is enormous and offers big saving possibilities in almost every product category. The category of MRO (maintenance, repair, and operations) products, worth $300 billion in the US, will be taken as an example to depict the potential value creation when switching from the "traditional" to the electronic marketplace. Even if only 10-20% of these products (that is $30 - $60 billion) were sold via electronic markets instead of through traditional channels, and the estimated savings of 10-20% are realized, a value creation of $3 - $12 billion is possible in just this product category.

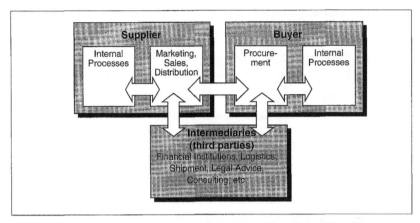

Figure 21: Buyers, sellers, and intermediaries (adapted from [Geba1998, p. 3])

A battle between buyers, sellers, and intermediaries to capture this value seems inevitable. Regardless of this, the emergence of electronic marketplaces offer rewards for every participant [Berr1998, p. 152]:

- **Sellers** can reach more customers, gather better information about them, target them more effectively, and serve them better.

- **Intermediaries** can earn transaction commissions and fees for value-added services such as information capture and analysis, order and payment processing, and consulting services.

- **Buyers** are able to compare products and prices easily and therefore compel suppliers to compete more fiercely than ever.

The electronic marketplace that is going to be observed more in detail in this thesis is based on Internet-Technology and Systems. This does not necessarily imply that the transactions between market players is done via the "open" Internet, but rather means that systems are based on Internet Technology, such as Web browsers or the TCP/IP standard.

Since the electronic Marketplace is very different from the "traditional" Marketplace, it does require a certain infrastructure and environment that enables Buyers, Sellers, and Intermediaries to participate and interact. Paper based catalogs used in the "traditional" marketplace for instance have to be replaced by electronic catalogs.

A number of software vendors and integrators with different approaches have recently sprung up to help buying companies as well as suppliers and intermediaries to establish this infrastructure and therefore enable them to participate in the electronic marketplace.

Especially for the procurement of indirect goods and services, which is the main focus in this thesis, a wealth of software vendors and integrators offer support for buyers, sellers, and intermediaries. Segev, Gebauer and Färber [Sege1998] identified 12 categories of business strategies that offer help in providing the necessary infrastructure for the different market participants. The following is a list of the identified categories with the most important vendors/ integrators in each group:

- Desktop purchasing systems (Commerce One, Ariba, Elekom/ Clarus, Concur)

- Enterprise resources planning (ERP) systems (Oracle, SAP)

- Supply chain management (i2, Manugistics)

- Electronic commerce platforms (Trade'Ex, Netscape)

- EDI/VANS providers, supplier ramp-up (Sterling, Harbinger, Commerce One)

- Outsourcing services (GEIS, Corpro 2000)

- Catalog and catalog management providers (Aspect, Harbinger, Requisite)

- Electronic market places (NetBuy, Digital.Market)

- Suppliers and sell-side solutions (Grainger, Intershop)

- Advice and implementation (Andersen Consulting)

- Payment services (Visa, American Express)

- Auctions and bidding services (Onsale, FreeMarket)

This categorization is just one way to gain an overview of the variety of approaches that are currently available to provide support in one way or another for the procurement of indirect goods and services. All vendors/ integrators try to help the buying companies, suppliers and intermediaries establish an infrastructure to shift day-to-day procurement activities from central purchasing to the end-user community [Sege1998]. They all share the objective to support the procurement of indirect goods and services through Internet based Technologies and System (ITBS) in order to address the main problems depict in chapter 3 that characterize the "traditional" procurement of indirect goods and services.

While some software vendors offer solutions like Desktop purchasing Systems (DPS) that are implemented on the buyer's side (buy-side), others target to help suppliers to set up electronic product catalogs on the sell-side. A third group does not actually offer applications and systems, but rather provides advice and help in implementing these systems.

For this thesis actually not all of the above-presented categories are relevant. Only those, which will be used further in this thesis, will be introduced more in detail in the following.

The objective in this chapter is to present the business model and main idea of the most promising and comprehensive Internet based Technologies and Systems currently available on the market that are able to support the procurement of indirect goods and services.

Electronic Product Catalogs (EPCs) and Catalog Management is outlined at first in section 4.1, because:

- They represent the most basic type of purchasing in electronic commerce [Comm1998].

- They are a key issue of electronic commerce,

- They need to be considered within several other approaches, like Desktop Purchasing Systems, where Catalogs are a core component, and

- They currently account for 60 percent of the online business-to-business market [Jahn1998, 54].

According to Geoffrey Moore, founder and chairman of the Chasm Group, "The catalog - not the lack of transaction processing software, not the lack of bandwidth to the home, not the lack of robust security, and not the lack of an appealing shopping experience - is what is blocking the growth of Internet commerce today" [Moor1999].

Besides Electronic Catalogs and Catalog Management, particular attention will be devoted to applications that are implemented at the buyer's side (see section 4.2). These are Desktop Purchasing Systems (DPS), which were among the first to provide comprehensive purchasing solutions and therefore gained much attention over the last month [Sege, 1998] and Enterprise Resources Planning (ERP) systems, which are recently targeting the procurement of indirect goods and services as well.

Other categories that are going to be presented in this chapter are:

- Outsourcing Services (see section 4.3), and

- Auction services (see section 4.4).

4.1 Electronic Catalogs and Catalog Management

Electronic product catalogs (EPC), or short Electronic Catalogs, are a key component of electronic procurement as they represent the most basic type of purchasing in electronic commerce [Comm1998]. According to Forrester Research, electronic catalogs currently account for 60 percent of the entire online business-to-business market [Jahn1998, p. 54].

Electronic product catalogs are information systems that put emphasis on the multimedia presentation of products (or services) and which contain some standard functionality of searching, selection, and ordering of products and services [Koch1997, p. 16]. Electronic Catalogs can be distributed via Discs, CD-

ROMs or the Internet. In this thesis the focus is on Internet-Technology based Electronic Catalogs.

They are the online parallel to traditional paper based catalogs but offer several new features and possibilities, such as continuos change and update of product availability and prices, enhancement of information through multimedia presentation of products, and different types of search mechanisms.

Without easy access to "good" catalog content – defined as accurate, up-to-date and searchable product information, an electronic catalog is worthless. Good content (and not volume of content) is the key to any Internet procurement solution [TPN1999]. Therefore content management is a critical process in the development of electronic catalogs and will be explained more in detail in section 4.1.2.

First however different Electronic Catalog options will be depict.

4.1.1 Electronic Catalog Options

Usually three different types of Web-based electronic catalog options are distinguished. Based upon who manages and hosts (stores) the catalog the three options are [Caff1997; TPN1999, p. 3; Shap1998, p. 33]:

1. **sellers** – sell-side electronic catalogs (see 4.1.1.1)

2. **Buyers** – buy side electronic catalogs (see 4.1.1.2)

3. **intermediary** (third party) – third party managed electronic catalog (4.1.1.3)

All of them are going to be explained more in detail in the following, highlighting the pros and cons of each approach.

Besides those three options, a new way of creating catalogs of products and suppliers **"on-the-fly"** using the eXtensible Markup Language (XML) will also shortly be introduced in section 4.1.1.4.

4.1.1.1 Sell-Side Electronic Catalogs

Electronic Product Catalogs that are offered by suppliers at their own Web site are called Sell-Side Electronic Catalogs. These suppliers usually manage the electronic catalog and content themselves or with the help of intermediaries (catalog management providers) like Aspect (www.aspect.com), Harbinger (www.harbinger.com), or Requisite (www.requisite.com). Some of the sell-side catalogs are Information only Web-sites other offer customized web sites with online ordering, payment, tracking capabilities, and even customized prices. Most of them offer a user-friendly environment where point and click icons make navigation easy and products can be configured according to the customers' need.

- **Information only Web-sites** (catalogs) are regular web sites accessible from every user with an Internet connection. Although, these pages mainly provide information about a company and their products they offer selected items with nonnegotiable prices and conditions. Buyers (end-users) can search the catalog and order these products.

- **Customized Web-sites solutions** are catalogs with specifically configured content and pre-negotiated prices. They can only be visited by certain companies (and users within the company) with access rights.

Even though this is a promising new selling channel for businesses, sell-side catalogs alone usually don't meet the needs of buying companies, because [TPN1999, p. 3; Caff1997, Shap1998, p. 34]:

- Buyers with hundreds or even thousands of suppliers do not have the resources or time to go out to every supplier's web site, each with its own look and feel and ordering process.

- Multiple systems must be learned, because every seller has a different user interface.

- Requisitioner must know which catalog to access.

- Only one supplier's catalog may be accessed at a time, which makes supplier, product and price comparison difficult.

- Most suppliers with Web-based electronic catalogs do not have in place the necessary mechanisms to display each particular buying organization's contracted item with negotiated prices, therefore buyer specific products and prices are not always available.

- Most oft them do not have mechanisms in place to control user access based on the corporate customer's business rules. Therefore, even if an employee order from the Web catalog of a preferred supplier, he or she may be ordering items without a corporate buyer's approval, or may be selecting supplies that are not part of the negotiated contract.

- Purchases from sell-side web catalogs are difficult to track and therefore do not provide buying organizations with the spending data needed to help them make strategic purchasing decisions.

Sellers, even though they have no core competence in hosting and maintaining catalogs, usually experience the following advantages when setting up a sell-side electronic catalog [Caff1997]:

- Low cost & easy maintenance, due to one system for all customers.

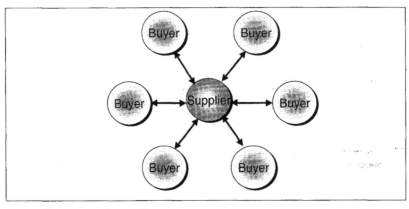

Figure 22: Sell-Side-Electronic Catalogs

Successful implementations of Sell-Side Electronic Catalogs are currently offered by such companies like Cisco (www.cisco.com), Grainger (www.grainger.com), and Dell (www.dell.com).

4.1.1.2 Buy-Side Electronic Catalogs

Buy-Side Electronic Catalogs are built and stored within the buying organization. Usually buyers manage the electronic catalog and content themselves or with the help of an intermediary. The application (software) runs locally on the company's information technology (IT) infrastructure – usually its Intranet – and can be accessed by employees using standard Internet browsers on their desktops. These catalogs contain data on all the products and services approved by the company through negotiated contracts and can streamline the requisitioning and ordering process, reduce contract leakage and enforce spending limits for employees [Shap1998, p. 34; TPN1999, p. 3].

While buy-side catalogs improve the purchasing process and give corporate buyers greater control over spending, their success depends very much upon the ability and cooperation of suppliers. They have to provide data (catalog content) in usable formats and update the information to reflect price and product changes [Shap1998, p. 34]. Therefore, usually intensive interaction between buyers and sellers is required [Sege1998, p. 11].

In this solution, supplier's product databases (not catalogs as a whole) are duplicated onto the buying organization and then exported into an aggregated database. The buy-side electronic catalog is therefore an **aggregated catalog** from several suppliers and product information is up-to-date only at the last database duplication-aggregation point [Agen1998].

This can represent a mayor challenge especially for large buying organizations, which often have supplier bases ranging from small operations with paper based catalogs to electronic commerce-savvy suppliers [Shap1998, p. 34]. In case buyers are not supported by an intermediary, they are left on their own to manage the content ramp up process (content acquisition), rationalize all of the various catalog formats that come in from suppliers, and deal with the many data quality issues that will undoubtedly arise. In addition, the "do it yourself" option can be prohibitively expensive due to heavy investments in software, hardware, and in-house personnel required to manage and maintain catalogs (create catalogs, store them, and keep all the information up-to-date [TPN1999, p. 4].

Due to the cooperation that is needed from suppliers and the resources that have to be in place, the buy-side catalog often is limited to large organization with sufficient buying power and budget.

Other pros and cons usually associated with the buy-side catalog are [Caff1997]:

Pros (Buyer's Perspective)

- Fast and easy product-centric search and selection
- Access to multiple supplier offerings
- Uniform system for all suppliers, therefore same look and feel

Cons (Supplier's Perspective)

Multiple catalog format support results in:

- Duplicate effort
- Complicated content management
- Increased costs

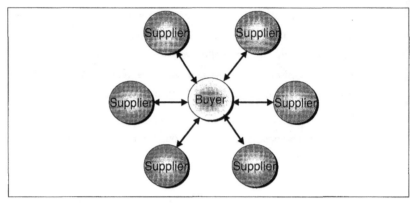

Figure 23: Buy-Side-Electronic Catalogs

4.1.1.3 Third Party Managed Electronic Catalogs

Third Party managed electronic catalogs (or Service based solutions) are the third web-based option of electronic catalogs. The main idea is to combine the benefits of the sell-side and buy-side catalogs without the problems associated with both of them.

In this option the electronic catalog is hosted and managed by a third party, which offers the (outsourcing) service to buyers and suppliers (see Figure 24).

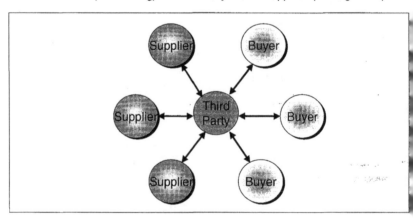

Figure 24: Third-Party Electronic Catalogs

The third party provides a **secure electronic marketplace service** that is shared by multiple buyers and suppliers (trading partners) [TPN1999, p. 4].

This model allows buyers to control employees' purchases while outsourcing the required services to a third-party organization that specializes in content and catalog management. By choosing an electronic marketplace service, organizations receive rapid access to a global marketplace made up of their preferred suppliers without any infrastructure costs or ongoing maintenance worries. True electronic marketplace service providers will handle the entire supplier engagement and acquisition process and host all supplier catalog content on behalf of the buyer and the supplier. Suppliers need to provide their catalog data only once, which can then be repurposed and supplemented with contract-specific information for each new buying customer that joins the service. In addition, supplier can easily access the service to make updated to catalog content online [TPN1999, p. 4].

Within the electronic marketplace, each buying organization has its own "virtual" private catalog that combines the product data and negotiated pricing (and contract terms) for preferred suppliers [Shap1998, p. 34]. In order to access the service, buying organizations simply need to provide a standard Internet browser to the end-user. Authorized employees are then empowered to search for and order contract items from pre-approved suppliers, giving them instant visibility to negotiated items and pricing [TPN1999, p. 4]. As of today, this model offers no configuration tool that allows the end user to build (assemble) his/ her own product according to specific needs. Purchases of PCs for example are not supported. Therefore, these products have to be pre-configured by the buyer in order to be incorporated into the catalog.

Some of the benefits, for both buyers and suppliers, are [Caff1998]:

- One system for all customers/ suppliers (one catalog format),

- Suppliers control catalog maintenance,

- Fast and easy in use,

- Shared cost between buyer and seller,

- Third party has core competence in catalog and content management.

4.1.1.4 XML and Catalogs "on-the-fly"

Until recent, the only available solution to integrate catalogs (product information) form different suppliers into a single buy-side catalog was through catalog aggregation (see 4.1.1.2).

However, using agent-based technology and the Extensible Markup Language (XML), buyers are now able to create customized catalogs of products and suppliers "on-the-fly". XML has the potential to solve to a large extend the problems associated with assembling (aggregating) catalogs from multiple suppliers that were mentioned in the previous sections.

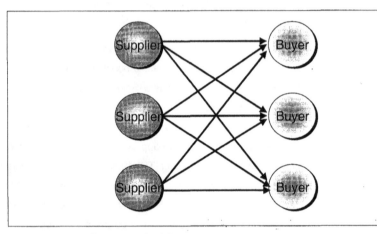

Figure 25: Catalogs "on-the-fly"

XML (eXtensible Markup Language) is a technology developed to upgrade the capabilities of the Internet for electronic commerce applications. Currently, HTML (Hyper Text Markup Language) is being used to format documents for display on Web-browsers. It uses a fixed, non-extensible grammar that allows almost anyone to publish information. The simplicity of HTML and the ability to hyperlink supported the rapid growth of the Web in the beginning [Färb1998, p. 47].

Since HTML was primarily designed for publishing information on the Web and not for describing the data maintained in a document, it is almost impossible to search and index these documents effectively. These shortcomings of HTML are one of the reasons for missing structure of the Internet and the limitations of search engines (agents) such as Yahoo or Lycos [Färb1998, p. 47].

HTML-documents are designed for human eyes because it makes them appear aesthetically pleasing on the Web. Therefore HTML based applications are most useful for business-to-consumer electronic commerce, where a human (end-user) interacts with the system through a Web-browser, browsing catalogs and placing orders. They are not the most effective design for business-to-business electronic commerce, because it does not offer the possible to query and manipulate the data in the documents and allow applications to application communication and integration [Webm1998].

Business to business electronic commerce is done between buyers, seller, and intermediaries using Internet-Technology and electronic commerce applications in order to execute electronic transactions, place orders, browse catalogs, monitor inventory levels, check the status of shipments, review account information, and conduct other operations. HTML is currently an impediment and limiting factor for this type of commerce, because the tags in HTML are too simple to encode the structure and the semantics needed for richly structured documents, databases, and catalogs [Webm1998].

XML deals with these limitations by making it possible to describe data maintained in documents, allow querying and manipulating of this content, and enable applications to exchange data in a usable format. It is very similar to HTML (and is in fact interoperable with HTML), but it does not rely on a fixed format. Instead, XML is a metalanguage that allows to design new tags. It is a self-describing data format that makes it possible for groups of people or organizations to create their own customized markup language for exchanging information in their domain [Byle1999].

An XML solution begins with a trading community agreeing on a common set of term that describes the products and services that are regularly exchanged within the community. For example, the computer industry, via an organization such RosettaNet, comes together to agree that a "laptop computer" is a class of product that has seven important attributes which can be indicated with a finite number of descriptive terms. The attributes might include: processor speed, screen size, RAM memory, disk memory, weight, etc. For each attribute including the product name, the supplier uses a common vocabulary of terms to describe the attributes: Think Pad, 366 mghtz, 8.0 gigabytes, etc. [Byle1999].

Now, the buying organization has a rich content source on its supplier's products and services that is organized by product class, and family. This will allow buying organizations to effectively obtain, compile, and maintain product catalogs and information from supplier organizations. It will enable buyers to create customized catalogs of products and suppliers either (1) through "on-the-fly" searches on the "open" Internet or (2) in a more controlled fashion with previously identified suppliers. In addition to exchanging product information content, XML will also form the basis for companies to send transaction messages (purchase orders, acknowledgements).

Ironside (www.ironside.com), Webmethods (www.webmethods.com) and AGENTics (www.agentics.com) are among of the first vendors to offer electronic commerce applications based on XML to support business-to-business electronic commerce.

Some benefits of this approach in comparison to the three traditional options of electronic catalogs introduced earlier in this chapter are [Agen1999]:

- The product information is obtained from right within the supplier catalog. Therefore instead of duplicating the catalog and updating it periodically, electronic catalogs are created dynamically and access the most up-to-date information source available in real time.

- Cost effective and convenient solution for both suppliers and buyer. Buyers are relieved from the tremendous effort of aggregating multiple catalogs onto their site, and suppliers are relieved from managing duplicated catalogs.

- No need of any type of intermediary in charge of content aggregation.

Since XML can address most of the issues currently impeding business-to-business electronic commerce many believe that is has the potential to become the de facto platform for electronic commerce.

However, in order to grasp these benefits, buyer need advanced software in place able to process XML documents and suppliers need to begin publish product information (content) electronically using XML.

Currently the lack of standards in product description represents one of the most important impediments for an appropriate use of electronic catalogs. This is irrespective of the type of Web-based electronic catalog used and therefore true for buy-side, sell-side and third party managed electronic catalogs, as well as for catalogs that are generated "on-the-fly".

Without easy access to "good" catalog content – defined as accurate, up-to-date and searchable product information, an electronic catalog is worthless. Good content (and not volume of content) is the key to any Internet procurement solution [TPN1999]. Therefore content management is a critical process in the development of electronic catalogs and will be explained more in detail in the following.

4.1.2 Content Management

Content Management, as the name implies, has to do with the handling of content or product information in electronic catalogs. It is a comprehensive process by which electronic product catalog data is gathered, organized, maintained, and presented for easy online purchasing. The time and effort required for this process is usually largely underestimated by many organizations. [TPN1999].

Without easy access to "good" catalog content (see previous definition) a company will never realize its true potential cost savings, despite any amount of reengineering the purchasing process.

The following is based on a White Paper from TPN Register [TPN1999], a joint venture of GE Information Service and of Thomas Publishing. Here, **several steps** that need to be followed in order to yield rich, accurate, and searchable catalog content that enables buyers to find the specific product they need easy and quickly, are outlined.

The complete process is known as "**data transformation**" and the idea is to develop electronic catalogs with usable content from existing data, like paper based catalogs. Depending on the quality of the existing data and the complexity of the files that are being created the process can cost several dollars per line item of product.

The **first step** in this process is to gather all computerized data available on a product. This can represent a mayor problem, because:

- Many suppliers do not have product data available in electronic form. In this case for example paper-based catalogs need to be converted into computerized formats. This is a manually intensive and very expensive process.

- Even when a supplier does have computerized product data, such information is often incomplete or indecipherable, and therefore unsearchable for buyers.

Figure 26 below illustrates the type of abbreviated data that one supplier might use to describe a particular type of item.

Part #	Product Name/ Description	UOM	Price
C1122973	6 XH BLK CS SMLS WELD CROSS SA234 WPB	EA	2690

Figure 26: Line item description

The **next step** in the process is to clarify the meaning of each abbreviation. The abbreviation "BLK" in the above diagram, for example, may represent the product's color, i.e., "black" or could mean "block". Therefore it is necessary to work back and forth with suppliers and have industry specific people doing this type of work. Unless the abbreviation is expanded or normalized, it is unusable in a buy-side electronic catalog or a third party managed electronic marketplace. The complete description of the above item, for example, is: "Extra heavy black carbon steel seamless weld cross SA234 weld fitting made from grad B material, 6 inches".

Once the data has been normalized, the **next step** is to load the information into specific fields in the product database that describe standard product attributes. This will enable to search and compare similar products quickly and easily.

The data transformation process is not complete until the product information is organized in a way that it assures maximum search flexibility. Therefore product categories have to be created using recognized industry specific terminology. Additionally, other categories can be created to meet the specific needs of a particular buying organization.

The data transformation process ensures that end-users can easily and quickly locate items within an electronic catalog. If buying organizations however want to leverage volume discounts, then contract terms, conditions and prices that have been negotiated with preferred suppliers, need to be incorporated. Regardless of the type of electronic catalog used, the system must offer an efficient way for suppliers to input pricing and contract term that they have negotiated with buying organizations.

Once the data within an electronic catalog is normalized and enriched with contract term and pricing, the information must be maintained on an ongoing basis. An electronic catalog system or service should provide an easy and flexible way of keeping data up-to-date, since prices and lists of available products can change sometimes daily. One way for ensuring the accuracy of product data is to provide suppliers with simple-to-use online tools for making frequent, small changes/ or changes involving a large number of products. Another way to do this is by creating these catalogs "on-the-fly", dynamically and in real time directly from the supplier (see 4.1.1.4 XML and Catalogs "on-the-fly").

4.1.3 Conclusion

This section presented at first different types web-based catalog models that can be differentiated based upon who manages and hosts the catalog. In addition to this, an innovative approach, using XML and agent based technology was introduced. Next, the content management issue was addressed, showing the complex process of data transformation.

For a buying organization to choose the right web-based catalog option will depend very much on the environment and the specific needs of the individual organizations. To succeed in choosing an appropriate e-commerce system, purchasing, IT, and management must study and understand not only the e-commerce application and the e-commerce system provider, but, perhaps even most importantly, they must assess their own company's readiness for online procurement. If, for example, a very high degree of supplier consolidation has taken place, then supplier managed electronic catalogs may be the answer. If it is desirable to use multiple suppliers and the ROI (Return on Investment) from automation is judged to be high enough to justify the additional costs, either a buyer or a third party managed catalog could be the right solution.

Whatever the choice of methodology, electronic catalogs are a major step forward especially for the procurement of indirect materials.

Nevertheless, there are still several barriers and obstacles that need to be removed and addressed until the full cost saving potentials of electronic catalogs can be realized. Especially in the area of catalog interoperability, which permits the mix of data from different sources of catalogs, much work remains to be done. In this field CommerceNet (www.commerce.net) is playing a leading role in the development and adoption of important industry standards and protocols, such as the Open Buying on the Internet (OBI) Standard (www.openbuy.org).

As shown in section 4.1.1.4 (XML and Catalogs "on-the-fly") big hopes and expectations are placed in the development of XML, which according to Patrick Gannon (Vice President Strategic Programs of the CommerceNet Consortium) will enable and support many new business models and dramatically change and shape the economics of Electronic Commerce in the future.

4.2 Buy-side Applications

In this section an overview of current buy-side applications will be provided. Buy-side applications indicate that the system providing support for business processes is implemented at the buying company. Among them are desktop-purchasing systems (DPS) and enterprise resources planning (ERP) applications, which will be of interest in this section. Desktop-purchasing systems are applications that automate and support processes for the procurement of indirect goods and services. Enterprise resources planning (ERP) systems in contrary consist of a number of modules, which address different business functions. In this case purchasing is just one of several supported functions and is mainly focused on the acquisition of direct (production oriented) goods and geared to support the professional buyer.

In the following the system functionality as well as strengths and weaknesses of DPS will be analyzed more in detail and possible overlaps and integration with ERP systems will be discussed. Most of the data used for this section is based on a research study (release 1999) by Judith Gebauer of the Fisher Center for Management & Information Technology at the University of Berkeley [Sege1998].

4.2.1 Desktop-purchasing systems (DPS)

Desktop-purchasing systems (DPS) are software applications that are implemented at the buyer company to automate and support the procurement of indirect goods and services. They support the decentralized end-user to purchase goods and services from pre-approved electronic catalogs and free purchasing personnel from day-to-day transactions. Customers are given a system that is easy to use, flexible and can be integrated with a company's existing IT infrastructure. The new approach and uniqueness of these systems is that they specifically target the end-user by providing a user-friendly interface. Furthermore, they can be used as **stand-alone systems** or **front-end application** with connection to an ERP system.

4.2.1.1 System functionality

Desktop-purchasing systems (DPS) enable end-users in buying companies to search in customized catalogs, route and track requisitions through the internal approval process, and order online from suppliers. Furthermore, they support purchasing activities such as product and supplier selection, requisitioning, purchase order processing, catalog update and content management, reporting of spending patterns and supplier performance.

In general, they (1) include different modules to support the buying process, (2) provide mechanisms to set up and maintain a multi-vendor product catalog and (3) contain administrative master data components serving as base for the system.

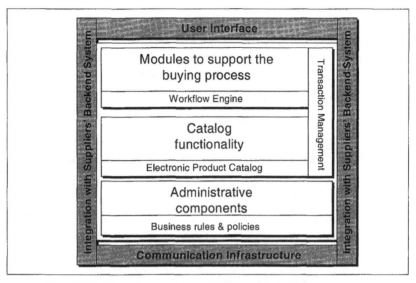

Figure 27: Modules and components of a Desktop Purchasing System (DPS)

(1)The modules that support the procurement process for indirect goods and services are Requisitioning and Approval, Order Creating and Submission, Receiving, Billing & Payment, Accounting, Tracking and Availability Checking, Reporting, and Delivery.

(2) The electronic product catalog is the core component in every DPS and a key issue in today's electronic commerce (refer to section 4.1). The integration of data from several suppliers into a unified structure is one of the most critical factors for the success of DPS. Electronic catalogs enable the end-user to search the electronic catalog with search engines (keyword search, search by attribute, browsing a classification tree) for standardized, pre-approved goods and services. However, there is no support for the configuration of complex items. Hence, so far DPS are not supporting purchasing processes that are more complex than simple catalog buying, such as RFP's, RFQ's or auctions. Furthermore, negotiations such as decision support or knowledge management is still not supported.

(3) Administrative components to set up and manage user profiles and business rules & policies are part of every DPS. Resulting, DPS provide purchasing with central control via the electronic implementation of business rules & policies while purchasing activities are shifted decentralized to the end-user requisitioners.

Besides these modules the systems provide tools to interface with the outside world. Such are *Transaction Management* for content uploading and transaction processing (e.g. purchase order submission, and payment transactions), and friendly *User Interfaces* which are important since the systems are targeted at a large number of end-users. Because of the friendly user interfaces, even non-technical and occasional users can operate the system and submit purchase orders. Thus, it is possible to "dis-intermediate" purchasing experts because the system supports the end-user throughout the entire purchasing process.

Furthermore, there is *Integration with Backend Systems* to exchange data with ERP systems and a *Communication Infrastructure* which is Internet-based for internal communication and Internet/ Extranet or VAN based for communication with suppliers.

4.2.1.2 Target customers

Most of the DPS target large companies since the systems ask for tremendous implementation and customization efforts, especially in cases where close integration with back-end applications is envisioned. As of now, DPS are still in the pilot stage, which makes companies implementing DPS first movers who receive highly customized and constantly upgrading applications. Therefore a premise for user companies is to have a sophisticated IT knowledge to deal with upcoming problems and interact with the application provider.

As mentioned above, electronic catalogs are a key factor for the success of a DPS implementation. They therefore require intensive interaction with suppliers who need to adopt with the electronic catalogs and provide their data in a specific standard. In fact, lack of supplier participation can make a DPS project rise or fall. The advantage of large companies is to be able to pressure their suppliers to participate. In contrary small or medium companies are depending on the supplier interest in participation. For those companies a sell-side solution or outsourcing agreement might be better, because of a lack of market power. Nevertheless, DPS can be used by small to medium size organizations, especially as stand-alone implementations in cases where and ERP system is not yet readily available.

Overall the extend of inefficiencies especially at large companies and sufficiently inefficient purchasing processes must be given to make the efforts of automating day-to-day operations and decentralizing procurement processes worthwhile.

4.2.1.3 Strengths and weaknesses

The strength of DPS is to focus on the end-users who requisition standardized goods and services from pre-approved electronic catalogs. Thus, DPS free central purchasing from non-value added day-to-day transactions. Therefore, the activities of the purchasing department will shift from transactional procedures to more strategic tasks like supplier sourcing and contract negotiations.

An additional advantage is that organizations can operate decentralized procurement by empowering the end-user while central purchasing personnel will maintain control since rules and policies are integrated in the DPS and therefore valid for all requisitioners.

Due to increased contract buying purchasing will be able to collect data to identify purchasing patterns, use volume discounts and reduce maverick buying. Using the data of purchasing patterns as well as advantages of increased contract buying and purchasing volumes will lead to a potential increase in purchasing power.

A disadvantage of current DPS is that a severe customization effort is necessary to get the system running. Every solution is individual and applied to the customer's needs since there is no generally accepted business practice established yet. Most of the implemented applications are still in pilot stage and new versions and upgrades are released constantly. This makes the users of the systems tester who have to adapt to constant change as well as improvements.

4.2.1.4 Overlap with enterprise resource planing (ERP) systems

DPS are often considered as the natural extension of ERP systems by providing the advantage of easy to use self-service front-ends. They address the problems of ERP systems for the procurement of indirect goods and services, because they have their core competency in this area. Furthermore they empower the decentralized located end-user by providing user-friendly access to the systems.

Recently ERP-vendors react to the request of easy to use self-service front ends and begin to introduce Web-based add-ons for their systems to support the procurement of indirect goods and services as well. Therefore, ERP systems are going to be introduced in the following with the main focus on their indirect procurement support.

4.2.2 Enterprise resource planning (ERP) systems

Enterprise resource planning (ERP) systems are the successor to materials requirement planning (MRP), which are software systems that resulted from requirements for greater control and efficiency in manufacturing systems. Early ERP systems were developed for manufacturing and production planning. The scope of the systems expanded to support functions, such as order management, financial management, warehousing, distribution production, quality control, asset management, and human resources management. Now, the systems concentrate also on "front-end" functions, such as sales force and marketing automation, electronic commerce, and supply chain systems. ERP implementations encompass the entire value chain of the enterprise, from customer management through order fulfillment and delivery.

4.2.2.1 System functionality

Enterprise resource planing (ERP) systems are complex software system connecting and automating basic business processes. For example, taking customers' orders, monitoring inventory levels or balancing the books. Data can be inputted through an accounting, manufacturing, or materials management system, nevertheless, ERP applications will automatically keep record of company's recourses such as raw materials and production capacity. This is done by digitally recording every business transaction a company makes, from the issuance of a purchase order to the consumption of inventory. Continually ERP are updating all connected systems to reflect each transaction. Thus, all users, from CEOs to buyers are all able to check with a single, real-time view their company's available resources and commitments to customers [Mina1998]. This is possible because the systems provide a unified information platform where theoretically everyone can access the same information throughout the entire company. Practically, the systems are lacking user-friendly front-ends and thus, severe training for the end-users is necessary to make the data available

Implementation of an ERP system involves a complex set of tasks, from selection and system design, to installation, tuning, maintenance and upgrade. Furthermore, business processes need to be improved when implementing ERP systems. Companies need to reengineer their critical supply chain business. This requires eliminating many non-value-added activities and creating a leaner, quick response order-to-delivery process. The technologies and capabilities needed to accomplish these tasks are often not obtainable in-house and therefore expensive consulting services are necessary whose fees can run as high as five to 10 times the price of the software. In addition implementation can easily last for 2-3 years or longer depending on the system's scope.

4.2.2.2 ERP procurement application

ERP consist of a modular approach, which provides applications for several business functions. Those modules are support e.g. accounting, sales, manufacturing, material management and procurement. In the case of procurement mainly professional buyers are addressed since the systems are too difficult to use for occasional users. In addition severe understanding of the supported business function is required, which leads to intense and costly end-user training.

For occasional end-users the systems are too difficult to operate. Even simple transactions such as filling a requisition or placing a purchase order conceal problems. Therefore ERP system vendors have started to implement easy to use self service front ends as well as providing tools for electronic commerce such as the possibility to establish electronic links with business partners, suppliers or third party service providers. But ERP vendors (like SAP) are too big to react fast enough to the market requirements. New start-up companies have therefore taken over the market of purchasing front-ends and Internet technology based procurement applications but will most likely be taken over by the much bigger ERP providers in the future.

ERP providers are slowly following the market of Internet technology based procurement applications for indirect goods and services. Nevertheless, they have the advantage to provide buying companies with compatible front-ends for the integration with already existing legacy systems. As an example for Internet technology based procurement support the advertised business-to-business procurement module of the German based ERP vendor SAP will be introduced more in detail.

Currently SAP owns the biggest market share of ERP systems and is recently trying to extend their ERP system (R/3) with a user friendly Web based front-end to support the procurement of indirect goods and services. Their objective is to automate business processes over the Internet with partner companies (Extranet), end consumers (Internet), and the company's own employees (Intranet).

Their B2B procurement solution consists of core purchasing related Internet Application Components (IACs), such as order with catalog, order service, change order, approval of requisitions, purchase orders, service requests, order status, receive goods, receive services and invoicing.

By introducing this procurement solution, SAP is extending its supply-chain optimization for requisitioning and purchasing non-production goods and services. Their efficient business-to-business procurement solution provides the buying organization with benefits, such as an user-friendly Web front end, real-time supplier integration and transaction cost reduction. Thus, end-users with little or no training are able to handle the complete procurement process, from creating a requirement to approving the invoice. Furthermore, purchasing personnel are able to focus on strategic sourcing and agreement negotiations.

So far ERP vendors are not the key market players in the area of Internet based procurement solutions for the purchase of indirect goods and services. Start-up companies, such as ARIBA, CommerceOne, Elekom, etc. who offer desk-top purchasing systems that can integrate with common ERP systems are leading the market right now. ERP vendors are not yet offering comprehensive front-ends for their ERP systems or applications that can be used as standalone systems. They are most likely going to take more time to develop front-end applications themselves or they will be taking over DPS vendors in the future to integrate their technology.

4.2.3 Evaluating Buy-Side Procurement Applications

In the following there is a brief outline of some considerations that should be taken into account when evaluating buy-side procurement applications:

- **Ease of use**: An automated procurement system can be a major force in consolidating purchases with approved suppliers. A system that is convenient, easy to use, and effective, quickly becomes the path of least resistance for employees to use.

- **Multi-vendor catalog capability**: A buy-side application should be able accommodate electronic catalogs from multiple vendors. That way it is possible to have one software product for all employee needs, rather than incurring the expense and effort of implementing different systems for different suppliers.

- **On-line ordering**: Ideally, ordering should be able to be handled in a variety of ways: by individual requisitioners; by administrative personnel ordering for others in their department; and by purchasing professionals. A user should be able to create and transmit an electronic order and have all of the approval routing, transmission, transactions, and financial settlement taken care of automatically.

- **Flexible routing and approval:** A system should provide a high degree of flexibility in preprogramming business rules and policies—what dollar volume requires authorization, which specific items or commodities require multiple signoffs, who has signature authority over what types of orders. The system should automatically route orders for approval and notify users of the status of their orders.

- **Multiple options for communicating with suppliers:** An automated procurement system should offer multiple ways of transmitting orders to suppliers: Internet file transfer, EDI (electronic data interchange), email and automated fax. This flexibility will maximize the options in selecting suppliers, and won't limit the search to those that use a particular type of technology.

- **Online customer service:** Users should be able to check the system directly to determine the status of an order. This automated customer service function will provide users with faster access to information, and minimize the time that purchasing department employees spend acting as "information intermediaries."

- **Financial settlement:** The system should automate the entire transaction cycle, from product selection through invoice matching and payment in order to have maximum impact on the total cost of procurement.

- **Reporting capabilities:** An automated procurement system should be able to track every transaction made through the system and report purchase

resources and competencies that make up the essence of the business, and outsource non-core resources and competencies to a third party [Kotl1997, p.66].

Especially in the area of procurement there are several circumstances under which some or all procurement activities would best be outsourced to an appropriate third party. Five different cases are therefore going to be introduced in the following [Port, 1997]:

Case one:

A company lacks in house technical expertise for the products or services being purchased. Therefore outsourcing procurement functions might be appropriate in circumstances where specific technical knowledge is required and when knowledge of products and services is very limited. Furthermore outsourcing might be beneficial if a company is taking on a new specialized product that requires extensive training and expertise to buy.

Case two:

Outsourcing is to consider if purchased items are low in value and/or standardized and where purchases are repetitive because of high frequency and volume. This affects procurement of standard, low cost, high volume parts, where few technical or quality issues are required. Commodities, which are characterized by every day, routine procurement processes are therefore especially suitable.

Case three:

In the case that companies lack buying power, outsourcing offers advantages. For example, purchase volumes can be increased by adding other company's purchases, which leads to more buying power. This is especially beneficial to small companies with limited buying capacity.

Case four:

Small sized companies who experience too high administrative costs who are lacking resources and whose internal purchasing costs are very high are likely to consider outsourcing.

Case five:

Outsourcing is to be considered as an option if an organization wants to acquire or get access to goods and services that are out of their price range, or where the associated cost of ownership can not be afforded. An example may be complex software applications like Enterprise Resource Planning (ERP) systems, which usually are limited to large companies with sufficient resources regarding budget, knowledge, and infrastructure.

4.3.2 Outsourcing degree

The level or degree of outsourcing pursued by an organization can differ considerably, therefore outsourcing needs to be differentiated depending on the degree of the third party participation. The two possible extremes are:

- No third party participation at all: no outsourcing

- 100% third party participation: outsourcing

Between these two extremes the range can vary from outsourcing of discrete parts or services to outsourcing an activity, or even an entire function [Ellr, 1997]. Figure 28 depicts these two extreme scenarios which will briefly be introduced in the following.

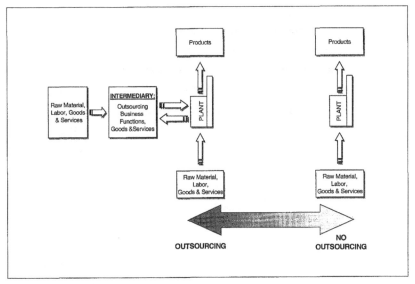

Figure 28: Outsourcing degree

On the right side of the continuum the buyer manages the procurement process without any assistance of a third party. Therefore the responsibility for the purchasing function remains at the buyer side.

On the left side of the continuum there is total outsourcing of processes, functions and/or goods and services. Organizations opting to outsource the procurement of certain items select and hire an integrator with expertise in materials management from outside of their company to manage the function for them. The third party is in charge of the procurement process form sourcing and requisition to payment and delivery. He manages the buying process, inventory, and supplier base, and provides a variety of other value-added services as well.

Between these two extremes are strategies that combine pieces of both. This option is attractive for organizations whose corporate culture is not ready for total outsourcing of the purchasing function. They usually outsource only certain items that are difficult to manage in terms of technical reasons [Aver, June 19, 1997].

4.3.3 "Traditional" and new outsourcing business models

There are different outsourcing business models that have to be considered in the area of indirect procurement. They can be distinguished according to a variety of factors, such as the kind of service that they provide, the parts of the process that they cover, and the degree of information system support that is involved [Sege1998]. In the following three different outsourcing models will be introduced. The "traditional" procurement outsourcing model will be presented first (see section 4.3.3.1), then outsourcing of procurement supporting Internet technology and systems will be introduced (see section 4.3.3.2) and in the end a business model that makes use of the combination of both approaches will be outlined (see section 4.3.3.3).

4.3.3.1 "Traditional" procurement outsourcing

In this case, a third party (outsourcer) is usually responsible for the entire purchasing function. They are in charge of the procurement process from sourcing and requisition to payment and delivery. The outsourcer manages everything, from picking up the approved requisition, to delivery and payment. Furthermore they select, negotiate and manage relationships with suppliers. They pay all invoices, so their clients accounts payable is left with just one payment to the outsourcer. Due to outsourcing the procurement activities the company can become more competitive by concentrating on their core activities. This solution does not require a sophisticated IT-infrastructure because information with the outsourcer can be exchanged using traditional channels of communication such as fax, phone or email. Therefore this type of outsourcing usually comes along with relative little use of Information technology.

A study conducted by Purchasing Magazine [Morg, 1998] identifies four major outsourcing categories in the context of indirect goods and services:

- General services, including cleaning, HVAC maintenance, machine maintenance, printing, and personnel services.

- Shipping and logistics services

- Safety products and services

- Stocking for general maintenance items, machine parts, bearings, electrical supplies, cutting tools, hand tools, and coating.

In general indirect goods and services have to be considered as being suitable for outsourcing, since they usually involve low risk and are not of strategic relevance for the business operation. Especially the procurement type of commodities seems to be best suitable for "traditional" outsourcing.

4.3.3.2 Outsourcing of procurement supporting Information Technology

In this business model the outsourcer provides the buying company with IT infrastructure and applications to support their internal and external purchasing activities. This type of outsourcing often requires changes (but not reengineering) of the procurement process at first, in order to make them suitable for the application or system. Unlike the "traditional" procurement outsourcing, there is no involvement in the actual day-to-day procurement process by the third party. The responsibility for the purchasing functions remains at the buyer side. This allows the company to focus on its core strategic purchasing activities such as sourcing for new suppliers, negotiating better contracts, manage supplier performance and analyze buying pattern of end-users, while the outsourcer provides the necessary IT infrastructure and is in charge of updating and maintaining the required software and hardware.

The IT infrastructure, that is the software applications and the hardware, can either be implemented at the buyer side or hosted by the outsourcer. Upcoming market players called 'Application Service Provider (ASP)' keep and maintain the IT infrastructure within their facilities and link users via dedicated lines or through the "open" Internet to their equipment and application. All IT related work, such as installations, upgrades, and maintenance is provided by the third party outsourcer.

The "networked economy" ends the need for data to reside in a specific physical location and therefore allows to have centralized application servers and database servers that can be shared by users around the world [Sim1998]. Among the applications that are already available and offered this way are Email applications, ERP applications and modules, and procurement applications. This will enable companies to gain access to applications that used to be out of their price range and change the way in which companies acquire this type of systems.

4.3.3.3 The innovative type of procurement outsourcing

Recently, a new type of outsourcers has emerged. They offer a combination of IT infrastructure and "traditional" procurement function outsourcing. This approach makes use of both of the above strategies and combines them in a broader and more comprehensive scope. In this case the outsourcer is responsible for the entire purchasing process and additionally provides the customer with necessary IT infrastructure and applications. Furthermore, the solution provider is responsible for reengineering the procurement process and the implementation of the systems and applications The implementation can be either done at the buyer side or hosted by the outsourcer.

The service provider operates and maintains the IT infrastructure, selects, negotiates and manages relationships with suppliers, and administers the entire process from taking and fulfilling requisitions to issuing authorizations for payment. The traditional procurement process will be reengineered in this case to suit the implemented IT-infrastructure and procurement strategy.

One of the most comprehensive outsourcers in this field combines IT application outsourcing with implementation, consulting, reengineering of business processes and education and training of purchasing personnel.

4.3.4 Considerations and Evaluation

Due to the nature of the subject and the uncertainties involved, outsourcing has to be considered a complicated and risky undertaking. Instead of managing internal functions and activities, outsourcing clients need to manage the relationship with third party service providers. Usually outsourcing contracts are long-term agreements and are quite complex in set up and management [Sege1998].

Since outsourcing is similar to the acquisition of a complex service (refer to section 3.2) requirements need to be defined in great detail, and potential outsource providers carefully selected (often based on trust) before any decision is made.

Other considerations that have to be taken into account are [Zens1994, p. 24]:

- Purchasing personnel might be reduced or appointed to new tasks.

- Close communication channels with the outsourcer need to be installed.

- Presumed non-strategic tasks and functions that might be easy to outsource today may become critical to the organization tomorrow. Therefore, to avoid lock-in situations with certain outsourcers contracts need to be reconsidered on a regular basis [Sege1998].

- The loss of flexibility, control, creativity, and learning skills in the outsourced business function [Sege1998].

4.4 Auctions

Auctions are gaining significant attention as a new way to buy and sell goods over the Internet. Anyone with an Internet connection can participate in a Web based auction. Therefore the potential participants of an auction are increasing in the same number as the Internet is growing.

This section will provide an overview about auctions as a mechanism to trade different kind of goods between sellers and buyers on the Internet.

After a short definition of the terms auction and online auction (section 4.4.1) the system functionality of auctions will be depict (section 4.4.2) and the impact of the Internet analyzed (section 4.4.3). The chapter will finish with an explanation of different types of auctions as well as the introduction of current Internet technology based business models and strategies (section 4.4.4).

4.4.1 Auctions and online auctions

An **auction** is an economic mechanism where buyers and seller(s) come together to determine the price of an item. One or more bidders (the buyers) and an item for sale are necessary for an auction. Usually the highest bidder will have to buy the item for the price he called out [Beam, Sege1998].

An **online auction** is defined as a web page, providing a neutral environment and displaying information about a good or service with the intent to sell it through a competitive bidding procedure to the highest bidder. The bidder participating in an online auction must have the ability to bid for items completely online although some online auctions allow telephone or in-person bidders to participate. Electronic delivery and payment is not essential for an online auction, although payment can be processed online by credit card and shipment can be provided electronically in case of a digital good [Beam, Sege1998].

As of today, Web based online auctions are mainly concentrating on selling goods from consumers-to-consumers or from business-to-consumers [Beam, Sege1998]. Recently, however, with the increasing use of Internet technology to simplify business operations, Business-to-Business online auctions gain popularity, too.

4.4.2 System functionality

Now, that the terms auction and online auction are defined this section will explain the system functionality of online auctions. Therefore the different participants of an auction are going to be introduced and auction rules and security issues discussed.

4.4.2.1 Participants and issues of an auction

The participants of an auction are the auctioneer, the buyer and the seller. The auctioneer is the central figure, because he provides the platform where buyer and seller meet.

In the figure below the participants of an auction are presented. Besides the auctioneer, the seller, the buyer and the trade object, **issues** such as auction rules, security, logistics and payment are of importance.

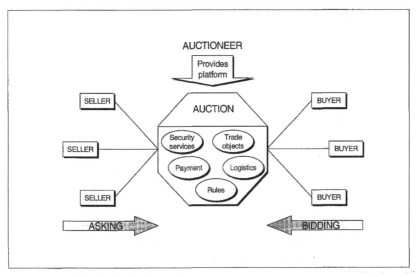

Figure 29: Participants of an auction

In the following the activities of the auctioneer, the buyer and the seller will be analyzed. In addition, trade objects will be listed and auction rules and security issues addressed.

Auctioneer: The auctioneer provides the institutional setting for the auction, that is, for the different transaction phases of the trading process: information exchange, price determination, trade execution and settlement. He can either be affiliated with the supplier or the potential buyer of the trade objects. However, most of them emphasize their role as intermediaries who provide trading platforms for a variety of buyers and sellers [Romm, Sudw1998, p. 52]. Auctioneers provide a platform for the connection of either many-to-many (buyers and sellers) or one-to-many (either the buyer or the seller is in plural).

Buyer: The buyer is the requesting party, who buys the product, traded in an auction. Buyers can either deliver bids for an offered item or receive offers regarding a tender. In an open online auction all people with access to the Internet are able to participate and offer bids.

Seller: The sellers are the offering party, who sell their products through an auction and ask for bids.

Trade objects: The trade objects are the goods and services traded on an auction platform between the buyer and the seller. The mechanism of an auctions is especially suitable for trade objects that are difficult to market via the established distribution channels, such as: [Romm, Sudw1998, p. 53]

- Products with a limited shelf life or last minutes products like seats in a scheduled flight, or golf tee-times,

- overstock products that are supposed to be separated from the new product series, and

- discontinued or reconditioned items.

Rules: Several rules have been developed to govern the trading process, especially the exposure of bids and offers and the trade execution. An additional set of rules governs the exchange and logistics of goods and payment. To observe these rules is meant to guarantee the correct execution of trades and is of the utmost importance in an electronic environment.

Security: Most online auctions, like any other online merchants can be considered safe places to shop. There is security through established and published rules and policies. Most Web auctions provide feedback system that let the participants review other people's experiences with a particular seller. In addition, they all support escrow services - third parties that act as intermediaries in transactions. For a commission (and possibly a small annual fee), an escrow service will accept payment from the buyer and hold it until the product is received in proper condition [Selz1999].

4.4.3 Advantages of the Internet

The impact of the Internet on auctions is gaining significance, because the number of potential participants of online auctions is increasing as fast as the Internet is growing. The high number of buyers and sellers using online auctions as well as the Internet technology offer several advantages compared to the "traditional" auction. Some of them are listed in the following [Lee1996, p. 401]:

- A global visibility of offerings due to a communication infrastructure with millions of potential trading partners.

- An increasing possibility of electronic product descriptions for trade objects due to standardized mechanisms for hypermedia representation.

- In the case of digital goods the entire trading cycle can be handled on the Internet.

- Reduced communication, information and search costs for the participants.

- Separation of the trading process and physical logistics of the trade objects for all non-digital goods.

- A reduction of coordination costs by allowing transactions to take place without the usual distributor. Fees for the auctioneer will be smaller than the margins of a distributor.

4.4.4 Types of online auctions

There are different types of online auctions depending on different auction mechanisms and players.

- **The Mechanisms** for online auctions are the same as for regular auctions and are based on the common mechanisms like the English auction, the Dutch auction, the First Price Sealed Bid auction and the Vickrey auction.

- **The Players** can be defined as the buyer and seller participating in an auction. The following constellations can be distinguished: Business-to-Business, Business-to-Consumer, and Consumer-to-Consumer.

In the following the different **auction mechanisms** will be explained briefly:

- The **English auction** is the most common type of auction. It is an open oral, ascending auction where the auctioneer begins at the seller's reservation price, and solicits progressively higher oral bids from the audience until only one bidder is left. The winner has to purchase the item, at the price of his last bid [Beam, Sege1998].

- The **Dutch auction** is common in the Netherlands. It is an open, oral, descending auction where the auctioneer begins with a price too high for anyone in the audience to pay, and progressively lowers the price until one bidder calls out, "Mine!" The winner has to purchase the item, at the price of his bid [Beam, Sege1998].

- The **First-price, sealed-bid auction** is common when auctioning off for example mineral rights. Bidders submit a single, irrevocable sealed bid which are opened simultaneously, and the winner is the highest bidder, who purchases the item at the price of his bid [Beam, Sege1998].

- The **Vickrey auction** lets all bidders submit a single, irrevocable, sealed bid which are opened simultaneously, and the winner is the highest bidder. He has to purchase the item at the second-highest bid price [Beam, Sege1998].

Now, that the auction mechanisms have been briefly depict, the different **player constellations** will be analyzed in the following.

- **Consumer-to-Consumer** auctions operate like flea markets. They bring individual buyers and sellers together and facilitate bidding, but don't have any role in completing the transactions or verifying the authenticity of the goods. Sellers describe their products and set bidding constraints, such as the minimum (reserve) price they'll accept for an item [Selz1999]. Basically Consumer-to-Consumer auctions provide neutral environments where buyers and the sellers can meet and trade goods.

- **Business-to-Business** or **Business-to-Consumer** orientated auctions sell merchandise from businesses to bidders. In same cases, first the auctioneer buys the trade objects from businesses and then acts as the seller in the auction.

In the following some examples for auctions with different player constellations will be presented:

- The online auction from **eBay** is based on an English auction mechanism and goods are traded between consumers (Consumer-to-Consumer).

- The online auctioneer **Onsale** is utilizing the English auction mechanism and goods are traded between businesses or from business to consumer. In this case, the auctioneer can also represent the seller and function as a business.

Since this thesis concentrates on **business-to-business** electronic commerce some exemplary online auction business models and strategies in this area will be introduced more in detail in the following:

- **FreeMarkets OnLine Inc.:** The approach of the start-up FreeMarkets differs from the regular auction platform in a way that they do not provide a neutral environment where sellers and buyers meet. Instead they help companies make decisions by providing three things: sourcing and consulting, an electronic commerce market system and information about the supply industries. FreeMarkets works out an exact product description with their client (the buyer) and then starts to search for a number of potential suppliers. The objective is to find suppliers with similar products and to eliminate all variables but price. The suppliers then will be invited to participate in a three hour online auction to determine the last open variable, the price. However, the best bidder (in this auction mechanism the lowest bidder) does not necessarily win the auction. That is because part of FreeMarkets consulting service is to choose the best supplier by counseling rejection of the lowest bid and recommending a supplier with better delivery system or long-term potential [Jahn1998].

FreeMarkets approach is targeting specifically large organizations (Fortune 500 companies) who are interested in trade objects such as semi-complex assembly parts (custom-engineered machine parts, metal stamping, iron casting).

However, this business model is not limited to these goods only. FreeMarkets business model is especially suitable for high value and complex items.

In order to make use of the auction model there has to be a competitive supply market of five or more variable suppliers that are able to meet the buyer's request. These suppliers can be located around the world and participate on the online auction from their desk-top PCs with a standard Internet connection.

- **FairMarket**

FairMarket hosts online auctions for corporate buyers of surplus lots such as PCs, electronic components, and chips. Their target customers are corporate IT departments looking for low end computing gear, as well as value added resellers and system integrators. Their approach will be explained briefly in the following:

Before FairMarket starts the auction they inspect the trade objects at a neutral Federal Express warehouse where the supplier had to ship the goods. The auction is then open for three days and the winning bidder will have 24 hours to transfer the money to a FairMarket's depository holding account before he receives the goods [Wild1997].

In the Figure 30 the auction mechanisms (listed on the abscissa) and the players (listed on the ordinate) are confronted. The figure illustrates that every mechanism can be matched with each player constellation. The above examples are integrated in the figure.

MECHANISM PLAYERS	English Auction	Dutch Auction	First Price Sealed Bid Auction	Vickrey Auction
Business-to-Business Business-to-Consumer	**Freemarket** **Fairmarket** **Onsale**			
Consumer-to-Consumer	**eBay**			

Figure 30: Types of online auctions

4.4.5 Evaluation

Internet based auctions offer advantages and possibilities for all participants but also include risks and uncertainties. Online auctions have low entry barriers for auctioneers, suppliers and buyers. Resulting, reputation for an auctioneer based on frictionless business operation is important to attract customers. High security standards are necessary to ensure that the traded goods as well as the transferred money reach their destiny. Therefore online auctions depend on their reputation, for example, whether the trading goods are available and of the promised quality, and weather trades are executed without friction. Reputations are different for expert and general public auctions.

Since set-up costs to run an auction are low, the transaction fees and commissions that are charged of buyers and sellers are small. In addition the sellers and the buyers have savings due to lower costs for the logistics of the trade objects as a result of the separation between trading process and physical logistic.

On the other side increased risks are obvious. Since in most cases (especially in consumer-to-consumer online auctions) the trade objects can not be inspected, undetected faults and poor quality of trading items may occur [Romm, Sudw, 1998].

5 Matching New Technologies with Procurement Types

In chapter 3 different types of procurement (commodities, services, and information technology) have been analyzed regarding their procurement processes and user requirements. Next, state of the art Internet based technologies and systems (IBTS) have been introduced in chapter 4 with the main focus on electronic catalogs, buy-side applications, outsourcing services, and auction models.

Therefore, the objective in this chapter is to match the introduced Internet based technologies and systems of chapter 4 with the outlined procurement types of chapter 3. The goal is to analyze for each procurement type potential IBTS for their procurement process support and discuss if and how they meet the identified user requirements.

To do so, first the procurement type of commodities will be matched with potential IBTS in section 5.1. Next, it will be analyzed if and how IBTS can support the procurement of services (see section 5.2). Finally, procurement of information technology, which is differentiated in hardware and software, will be matched in section 5.3 with promising IBTS to analyze their potential impact.

5.1 Commodities

Commodities were introduced in chapter 2.2.3.1 as tangible items of low value, low risk, high transaction frequency, high substitutability, and low product complexity, which are charged to an expense account within the month they are purchased.

Generally about 80% of an organization's purchase orders are for these low value items that constitute only for 20% of the purchased value. Adding the fact, that it usually costs between $25 and $250 to process a purchase order regardless of the item's value, illustrates the saving potential in this type of procurement when driving costs out of the procurement process.

As analyzed in section 3.1 there are certain requirements to improve the procurement process and to take advantage of the saving potential. The process needs to be simplified and automated as much as possible. Paper forms to exchange information need to be eliminated and the activities in which the purchasing personnel is involved have to change to more value-adding tasks. Overall the objective was to minimize transactions costs by streamlining the procurement process.

To achieve this goal, the possibility to support the procurement process by Internet based technologies and systems was mentioned. However, these systems have to support certain requirements deriving from the procurement process. Functions such as user friendly interfaces, easy to search electronic catalogs, integration with existing data systems and payment support among others (refer to section 3.1.4) were demanded.

Ideally, Internet based technologies and systems should simplify the procurement process and provide support from the definition of need to payment and after sales service. This means that every single step in the procurement process has to be electronically supported by some system components.

Current comprehensive solutions such as desktop purchasing systems (DPS), enterprise recourses planning systems (ERP), outsourcing services, "sell-side" and "buy-side" solutions, and auction & bidding models were introduced and analyzed in chapter 4. However, not all of them meet the special requirements of purchasing items with the specific characteristics of commodities. For example, auction & bidding models do not support a decentralized end-user request. ERP systems are not user-friendly and mainly focus on the buying professional instead of the occasional end-user.

The analysis of the introduced solutions (see chapter 4) showed that the most comprehensive system, coming close to the presented ideal scenario seems to be the implementation of a desktop purchasing system (DPS). Other promising solutions who have the potential to support the procurement of commodities are outsourcing services and supplier sell-side solutions. Outsourcing services

simply move all responsibilities and problems to a third party with more expertise in this specific procurement area. Sell-side solutions support the procurement process with entries to multiple electronic catalogs by using a simple Internet connection.

Thus, the following interesting approaches are going to be analyzed regarding their support for the procurement process:

- Desktop purchasing systems (DPS), section 5.1.1
- Outsourcing services, section 5.1.2
- Supplier sell-side solution, section 5.1.3

The objective in this chapter is to analyze and evaluate, if and how the above listed Internet based technologies and systems can meet the user requirements derived from the purchasing process of commodities as well as discuss weaknesses and changes.

5.1.1 Desktop purchasing systems (DPS)

In chapter 4.2.1 desktop purchasing systems were introduced as software applications especially designed to support the procurement of indirect goods and services. The question arises if these applications are able to address the different needs of organizations regarding the procurement process of commodities and if DPS are suitable for any company.

In the following section it will be discussed what kind of organizations are suitable to introduce a DPS see section 5.1.1.1 and the requirements to implement the systems will be depict. Furthermore, the support of DPS for the procurement process will be shown (see section 5.1.1.2), and the organizational and personal changes (see section 5.1.1.3) that are most likely going to occur in case of an implementation are going to be analyzed. To finish this section current weaknesses and problems arising from the implementation and use of the system will be listed.

5.1.1.1 Organizations suitable to implement a DPS

This section will show the requirements an organization has to fulfill in order to be suitable to implement a DPS. Resulting from the analysis in chapter 4.2.1, DPS require a significant amount of implementation and customization effort. They are not off the shelf applications and require severe changes within the organization. Procurement processes usually need to be adapted in order to meet the needs of these systems. Furthermore, the cost for consulting and implementing those applications can range from several hundred thousand dollars up to several million. Therefore the potential users of DPS are limited and need to fulfill certain criteria in order to be able to finance and implement such a project. DPS solutions as they stand today are well suited for companies that fulfill the following requirements:

- Existing processes must be sufficiently inefficient to pay off for the high implementation costs of DPS.

- Enough resources, regarding finance, infrastructure, manpower and knowledge have to be in place.

- Sufficient commitment/ openness towards new technologies and the readiness to change and reengineer procurement processes.

- Adoption of the system by a company's business partners (connectivity with suppliers) and integration and maintenance of supplier product data in a unified catalog structure.

System adoption by business partners is a critical factor to consider when implementing DPS because of the close interaction that has to be in place with participating suppliers. Therefore supplier cooperation is a key factor for implementing DPS. Product data from all suppliers need to be integrated in an electronic catalog that needs to be maintained on a frequent basis. The external factor – **buying power** - will impact on how the application will be designed and how the supplier will be integrated and participate in this solution. In addition, a

company's buying power has impact on how electronic catalogs will be organized.

- **Great buying power** gives a company the opportunity to host the electronic catalog themselves (buy-side catalog), run it on their company's information technology infrastructure and select suppliers according to their participation. The catalog contains data on all products and services approved by the company through negotiated contracts. Therefore, the end-user can search in a uniform catalog structure, with the integrated data of all suppliers. More information regarding buy-side catalogs is outlined in section 4.1.1.2.

- **Less buying power** indicates that the buy-side catalog is not a viable option, because suppliers cannot be forced to participate and provide data. Therefore, the two other options (sell-side catalog, third party managed catalog) are more suitable and need to be considered. The sell-side catalog is managed by the supplier and linked with the buy-side through an Internet connection. Third party catalog managers are intermediaries who are specialized in setting up catalogs and integrating product data from multiple suppliers (e.g. TPN Register). More information regarding these two options is provided in section 4.1.1.

Overall large corporations with readiness to change processes and organizational structures seem to be most suitable to implement DPS, because they meet the requirements best. Furthermore the ability to invest often decides upon size and depth of an application. Therefore most of the projects that are today in pilot stage are from large, innovative companies (Fortune 500).

However, DPS are not limited to large companies only and therefore implementations for small companies are possible, too. Often those companies don't have purchasing departments with adequate personnel and therefore are looking for process automation. Their ability to invest might be much smaller, but their flexibility to change processes and their openness towards new technologies is their advantage. Therefore, time for the implementation of the systems is short and the ROI is foreseeable.

5.1.1.2 Procurement process support and change

This section will analyze, if and how desktop purchasing systems can meet the requirements derived from the procurement process of commodities (see chapter 3.1). Furthermore, their potential to automate and streamline the process will be discussed. Therefore, each step of the procurement process will be discussed and changes analyzed.

Definition of need (information): Product selection can be executed and simplified through electronic catalogs providing strong search engines that search by item number, keywords or attributes. They have the advantage that end-users will not get frustrated searching and requisitioning items they need and in addition the catalogs provide the end-user with up to date content and product prices. The end-user will face an user-friendly front-end to enter the catalog, where multimedia presentation of content is possible. The description of need will become unnecessary since the product specifications are available throughout the system.

Requisitioning: End-user are able to choose items from aggregated supplier catalogs and state requisitions through the system. Issuing the requisition, they provide the system with such information as for whom the item is requested for, where it should be shipped, and to which account it should be charged. This eliminates the need for paper requisitions. Furthermore, data from the purchase request can be used for the purchase order, which reduces the need of multiple data entries and to duplicate data.

Approval: Purchase requisitions can be sent electronically for approval (if necessary). Consequently the authorized manager will automatically be notified of the waiting request. The application is able to designate alternative approvers through a pre-defined path in case the authorized manager is not available. Limits for necessary approval can be set. For example, any amount not exceeding $X does not need to be approved. After the authorized manager has approved the requisition, the end-user will be notified that his request has been sent to purchasing for order placement.

Purchase order: The system automatically releases the purchase order after the requisition is approved. Purchasing is allowed to combine line items from many purchase requests onto a single purchase order or issue many purchase orders from a single request. Furthermore, they can electronically "sign" purchase orders and send them to vendors through EDI, fax or over the Internet.

Delivery: Once items are delivered, the receiving department changes the status of the P.O. to "received" and the requisitioner receives a notification via e-mail.

Payment functionality may be included in the system (automatic matching of invoice and P.O.) as well, which enables users not only to pay but also to create and process invoices, payment authorizations, cost corrections and accruals. It also compares payment information with recorded rejections to ensure that the organization does not pay for damaged goods or standard services.

As shown above, DPS provide the functionality to support, automate and simplify the procurement process in every single step. End-users are able to search in up-dated electronic catalogs instead of using old paper catalogs. They do not need to invest anymore time in writing and processing descriptions of need and purchase requests. Purchasing personnel does not need to interact in the operational process anymore, such as purchase order sending or approval and order tracking. Furthermore, invoice matching and delivery is organized by the system.

The changes deriving from implementing a DPS and supporting the procurement process regarding purchasing organization and personnel will be analyzed more in detail in the following. Furthermore, the impact for the end-user and the budget holder will be discussed.

5.1.1.3 Organizational and personal changes

Implementing a DPS to support the procurement process comes along with significant personal and organizational changes within a company. Therefore, this section will analyze these organizational changes for the purchasing department and the changes in activity for the end-user, the purchasing personnel and the budget holder.

Organizational changes: Implementing DPS leads to organizational changes such as establishing an infrastructure that can help companies to decentralize purchasing activities. This means that some, or all, day-to-day purchasing operations shift from central purchasing to the decentralized end-user community [Geba1999]. Before the implementation of DPS decentralized buying request were leveraged and executed centralized by the purchasing department. Now, purchase orders are leveraged automatically because end-users order from a centrally established catalog with pre-selected products and prices.

A change in organizational structures always leads to significant changes in activities for the persons involved. Therefore the change in activities of the end-users, the purchasing personnel and budget holder will be addressed more in detail in the following.

End-user: The end-users will receive empowerment because of the shift from a centralized to a decentralized purchasing environment. All end-users have access to the system, the electronic catalog and therefore the possibility to initiate purchase orders regardless of their location within the company. They perform all procurement activities electronically and have access to catalogs with pre-selected and pre-priced products from defined suppliers. Basically, the company puts contracted suppliers at the employees' fingertips with up-to-date product description and pricing [Geba1999].

Purchasing personnel: Desktop-purchasing systems free purchasing personnel from their day-to-day activities by letting the end-user proceed the actual buying. Due to the empowerment of the end-user purchasing is able to concentrate on more strategic, value adding tasks such as supplier management, supplier performance analysis, spending pattern analysis, and negotiating agreements and contracts. Purchasing is free to manage the process, rather then to process its transactions [Caff1998].

Since the end-user is selecting and ordering items from the company wide catalog and initiating purchase orders, catalog setup and maintenance become critical success factors. Therefore, new activities for the purchasing personnel arise. For example, they are now responsible for catalog management such as content and price up-dates and supplier data integration. How complex and time consuming these new activities can be has been outlined in detail in section 4.1.2, content management.

Budget holder: The budget holder is participating in a simplified approval process. Email provides the ability to contact authorized management for approval everywhere and anytime. The improved workflow speeds up the approval process and therefore the time between sending the purchase request and issuing the purchase order can be reduced.

5.1.1.4 Weaknesses/ Problems

There are still several challenges that need to be met by DPS in order to provide a comprehensive solution for the procurement of commodities. Right now, there are no solutions available that suit every company, meaning that almost all applications are customized. This leads to significant implementation efforts. Although, not only the implementation of the new system but also the integration with the corporate IT infrastructure demands resources such as man-hours, licensing fees, hardware costs and training. Furthermore it is to consider that integration and links with ERP systems are complex [Sege1998].

The implementation of desktop-purchasing systems demands at least an adoption of the current procurement process. However, automating existing processes does not capture the entire potential of the systems. Processes need to be reengineered and streamlined before the implementation to provide the expected success.

Critical is the adoption of the system by suppliers. As already mentioned product data from suppliers need to be integrate in electronic catalogs. Those companies who have great buying power can force their suppliers to participate and implement the catalogs within their own system. Companies who lack buying power have to rely on sell-side catalogs or use intermediaries for catalog management.

Electronic catalogs are the key factor of today's DPS and a critical issue itself. Many companies underestimate the complexity of content management as well as the time to set-up and maintain the catalog. More details regarding electronic catalogs are outlined in section 4.1.1, electronic catalog options.

5.1.2 Outsourcing services

In the previous section DPS was analyzed as a comprehensive system to support, automate and streamline the entire procurement process of commodities. But DPS systems are not the only potential solution. Outsourcing services have become a recognized management option in the last decade and their significance even raised with the use of Internet related technologies such as Internet, Extranet, and Intranet. Therefore, this section has the objective to specifically analyze the support of outsourcing services for the procurement of commodities.

In section 4.3.1, different reasons for outsourcing have been introduced for different products and companies. Resulting, items are especially suitable for outsourcing, that are of low value and purchased in high frequency such as commodities. Furthermore, the characteristics of high standardization and non-strategic qualities have been pointed out.

In addition, companies need to determine the degree of outsourcing they want to acquire and select a strategy. They can either opt for traditional outsourcing, for outsourcing services to support Information Technology infrastructure or for an innovative type of outsourcing, which combines the two previous strategies (refer to section 4.3.3) for more details on different outsourcing strategies). Their support for the procurement process of commodities will be analyzed in section 5.1.2.1. Furthermore, organizational and personal changes deriving from the outsourcing service will be depict in section 5.1.2.2 and a conclusion with weaknesses and problems presented (see section 5.1.2.3).

5.1.2.1 Procurement process support and change

The different outsourcing strategies (see section 4.3.3) effect the procurement process of commodities in different ways. Therefore, each strategy's impact of the process will be analyzed separately and discussed in the following

1. The **traditional procurement outsourcing** covers and takes over the entire procurement process. Consequently, the responsibility for the procurement of commodities is delegated to a third party, which manages the process from picking up the approved requisition, to delivery and payment.

   End-users define their needs and send purchase requisitions to the purchasing department for approval. Once the requests are approved, purchasing forwards the purchase request to the outsourcer. Now, the service provider sources for items, selects suppliers, negotiates prices and manages the delivery terms. In addition, they are responsible for invoice matching and payment and leave their client's accounts payable with just one monthly payment for the service. Since this outsourcing service frees the purchasing department from most day-to-day transactions (except approval and requisition transfer) they are now able to concentrate on more strategic, value adding activities.

   This solution does not require a sophisticated IT-infrastructure because information with the outsourcer can be exchanged using traditional channels of communication such as fax or phone.

2. In the case of **outsourcing procurement supporting IT** the outsource service provider is responsible for the implementation and maintenance of the procurement application as well as supporting technologies such as email, Internet-, or Extranet-connection, but does not get involved in the actual procurement process. This means, the responsibility for the procurement of commodities remains at the buyer side.

117

In this case the support for the procurement process is similar to the support a DPS system is providing. The process can be automated and streamlined for efficiency. End-user will be empowered by searching electronic catalogs, issuing purchase orders and executing payment. Consequently, purchasing personnel will be able to concentrate on more strategic activities. Refer to section 5.1.2.1 for more details of the support of IT based procurement systems for the procurement process.

3. **Innovative outsourcing** supports the procurement of commodities by taking over the responsibility for the procurement process as well as setting up the necessary IT infrastructure and applications. The service provider not only operates and maintains the infrastructure, but also reengineers the procurement process to suit the IT infrastructure and procurement strategy. Furthermore, he selects suppliers, negotiates contracts and prices and arranges delivery and payment.

The decentralized located end-user connects to the system, searches electronic catalogs and defines his need. The following steps of the procurement process will be operated by the procurement system (refer to section 5.1.1.2).

Currently, one of the most comprehensive outsourcers combines IT application outsourcing with implementation, consulting, reengineering of business processes, and education and training of purchasing personnel. The business model is shown in Figure 31.

A solution is designed which will link the outsourcer, the supplier and the buyer (of the outsourcing service) on a unified platform. The result is a seamless tracking system in which buyer codes, account codes, the community structure, and catalogs are all standardized to make the procurement process efficient and measurable in its effectiveness. The IT infrastructure can either be implemented at the buyer side or hosted by the outsourcer.

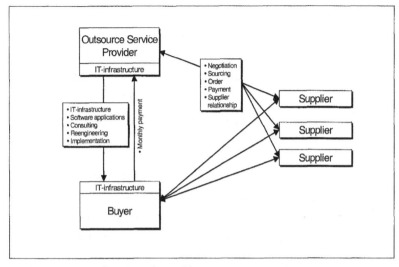

Figure 31: Innovative outsourcing model

To illustrate this outsourcing model a case study of organization B (Buyer) and organization O (Outsource Service Provider) is presented in the following:

Organization B has an outsourcing agreement with organization O for the procurement of commodities. O is provided with a contract to perform sourcing and procurement utilizing a fully integrated online purchasing and payment system. Organization O will maintain and operate the web-based system, select, negotiate and manage relationships with suppliers, and administer the entire process – from taking and fulfilling requisitions to issuing authorizations for payment. However, the outsourcer does not leverage its purchasing power, i.e. suppliers for O's outsourcing contractors are handled separately from their own contracts.

Within this solution electronic catalogs are maintained at the supplier side and are accessible via an Extranet. In addition, organization O has an application to provide unified access to catalogs of different suppliers, although O opts for single sourcing contracts.

5.1.2.2 Organizational and personnel changes

Different organizational and personnel changes within the buying organization come along with all three outsourcing strategies. Overall, purchasing personnel will receive new responsibility, which is the management of the outsourcing agreement for the entire duration of the contract.

1. In case of the **traditional outsourcing** strategy the procurement activities are taken over by the outsourcer. This excludes the buyer from the procurement process of commodities and the involvement in day-to-day purchasing activities, such as submitting purchase orders or invoice matching and payment. The end-user simply transfers his approved purchasing request to the service provider and instead of contacting the purchasing department for order tracking he is connected directly with the outsourcer.

   Purchasing personnel is now responsible for managing the outsourcing agreement. They are monitoring the outsourcer's performance and making sure that the conditions of the service agreement are met.

2. **Outsourcing of the IT-infrastructure** will have a supportive effect for the procurement department. The personnel will be free of clerical work, because processes will be automated to a great extend. Purchasing personnel can now concentrate on strategic tasks such as supplier sourcing, negotiation and contracting. Furthermore, they have the aggregated buying data to create spending patterns and make use of their increased purchasing power due to leveraged purchasing and contract buying. Refer to section 5.1.1.3 for more details on organizational and personal changes due to Internet supported procurement systems.

3. **Innovative outsourcing** will not only take over procurement processes but also reengineer and redesign them. Therefore, the buying company gives away the non-critical operation of buying commodities and concentrates now on more strategic, value adding tasks. Since this outsourcing is a combination of the previous strategies, the changes for the end-user and the purchasing personnel are similar to the above presented.

A critical issue of this outsourcing model is the management and the location of the electronic catalog. They can either be located on the buyer-side, the supplier side, or managed by a third party catalog provider. Refer to section 4.1.1 for more details on catalog management.

5.1.2.3 Conclusion

Resulting from all three outsourcing strategies (traditional procurement outsourcing, outsourcing of procurement supporting Internet technologies & systems and innovative type of outsourcing) there is a change in activities for the purchasing personnel. They are free from day-to-day operational activities and are now able to concentrate on more strategic tasks such as supplier sourcing, negotiation, contracting, and aggregating data to create spending patterns.

On the other hand, purchasing personnel will receive new tasks and responsibility. They have to manage the outsourcing agreement, monitor the outsourcer's performance and make sure that the conditions of the outsourcing agreement are met.

5.1.3 Supplier and sell-side solutions

In the two previous sections of this chapter the support of desktop-purchasing systems (DPS) and outsourcing services for the procurement of commodities has been analyzed. Now, this section will focus on supplier sell-side solutions.

Regarding to a recent study of Forrester research supplier sell-side solutions will have increasing revenues in commerce software licensing fees. The research center predicts a raise of 37% ($724 million) by the year 2002 [Dolb1998]. Consequently, an increasing number of suppliers are implementing sell-side catalogs to offer their products to an increasing number of users. Therefore, the objective of this section is to analyze if supplier sell-side solutions (supplier sell-side catalogs) are able to support the procurement of commodities and meet the requirements that have derived from the purchasing process in chapter 3.1.3.

First, sell-side catalogs will be introduced in section 5.1.3.1 and the then the two different options briefly outlined with regard to the procurement of commodities. Both solutions are then going to be analyzed for their procurement process support as well as their strengths and weaknesses (see section 5.1.3.2), before a conclusion in section 5.1.3.3 will end this chapter.

5.1.3.1 Different sell-side solutions

Supplier sell-side solutions are electronic catalogs offered from suppliers and implemented at the supplier side. They are integrated in the supplier's information technology infrastructure and can be connected via Internet or Extranet (refer to section 4.1.1.1).

In opposite to a desktop-purchasing system, supplier sell-side catalogs cannot be considered as comprehensive solutions because they do not provide end-to-end support for the procurement process. Mainly the steps of information (with product selection) purchase order and payment are supported. Furthermore, the buyer has to depend on the supplier to maintain the catalog content.

Supplier sell-side solutions are especially suitable for small to medium companies that do not have the resources to implement a comprehensive procurement system such as DPS but are looking for an inexpensive foray into online buying.

As introduced in section 4.1.1.1 two different sell-side solutions can be distinguished. There is the **information Web site**, which can be accessed by any public individual with an Internet connection and the **customized Web site**, which is password protected and is displaying specific configured content to meet the customer's needs.

Next, the information Web site as well as the customized Web site will be analyzed with regards to their support for the procurement process.

5.1.3.2 Procurement process support

This section will analyze the support of information Web sites and customized Web sites for the procurement process of commodities. Since supplier sell-side solutions are not comprehensive end-to-end procurement solutions the process will not be separated in the singles procurement process steps as introduced in chapter 3.1.3.

Information Web sites: Information Web sites (catalogs) are accessible from every end-user with an Internet connection. Buyers (end-users) can search the catalog and order offered products with fixed prices. In this case the end-user is limited to the product selection that the supplier offers and prices are nonnegotiable.

A weakness of this solution is that end-users have access to multiple sell-side catalogs and therefore, have to get used to different "look & feel". They have to adapt to different interfaces and utilize different search engines. Access to multiple catalogs makes it difficult to compare products and prices because the catalogs can only be entered one at a time. Therefore, displaying similar products of different brands at the same time is not possible.

Furthermore, company's business rules & policies cannot be implemented in the sell-side catalog. Organizations loose control over their end-users, which have easy access to a variety of catalogs. They can therefore circumvent the in-house procurement system and start maverick buying, which is equal to off-contract buying, because the end-user is not buying pre-selected items with pre-negotiated prices from preferred suppliers. End-users purchase regarding to there needs and often pay with their private credit card to then later ask for reimbursement. As already mentioned in the previous section (5.1.3.1) this problem is referred to as contract leakage.

Off-contract buying also takes the advantage of monitoring buying habits. Purchasing personnel will not be able to collect data to create spending patterns. In addition, it is not possible to leverage purchase orders and use high order volumes to receive discounts. Consequently, the company will loose buying power.

Purchasing departments are looking for solutions with end-user buying control that enable end-users to select contracted goods, issue purchase orders, and execute payment. Furthermore, they want end-users to select items from pre-configured catalogs with pre-negotiated prices.

As shown in the following, customized Web sites have the potential to address some of the above mentioned problems.

Customized Web sites: Customized sell-side solutions are catalogs with specifically configured content and pre-negotiated prices. They address many of the problems associated with information Web sites, and can therefore be considered as more comprehensive solutions.

Once the end-user is connected to the password and login protected catalog, search engines are available to provide easy access for products and information. This content is especially configured for the buying organization and even specific for each end-user. In addition to pre-selected items and prices, business rules & policies can be integrated for more end-user control. Resulting, the customization of the catalog for the end-users make approval processes unnecessary, because content and prices are already approved, before the integration in the catalog.

Customized catalogs do not only have the advantage of pre-selected items with pre-negotiated prices but also provide the purchasing department of a buying organization with data to create spending patterns. Furthermore, they ensure that end-users purchase only from preferred suppliers and buy contracted items. This way volume discounts can be achieved and buying power increased.

5.1.3.3 Conclusion

Two options of supplier sell-side solutions have been outlined and analyzed with the result that especially the customized Web site represents an interesting alternative for comprehensive DPS.

There are advantages and weaknesses of both sell-side solutions compared to a desktop-purchasing system, which will be briefly summarized in the following.

- The **advantage** of sell-side catalogs is that this procurement solution is much cheaper to implement than a comprehensive DPS, because sell-side catalogs are easy to access with a basic Internet connection.

  Catalogs and therefore content management is in the responsibility of the suppliers. Buyers do not face the problem of time and personnel consuming catalog set-up and content maintenance.

- The **weakness** of sell-side catalogs is that buying organizations have less control of their end-users. Especially the information Web sites inherit risks that end-users purchase off-contract, which makes it difficult to track spending patterns and increase buying power.

  Suppliers often lack of enough capacity and mechanisms to display every single item for the contracted customer. Consequently pre-selected and pre-priced items may not be available at any time.

  Catalog management is the responsibility of the supplier. Therefore, companies have to rely on the supplier to always provide the latest product and price updates.

5.2 Services

The procurement of services was differentiated throughout this thesis into routine services and complex services. Both are going to be addressed in the following with regards to if and how Internet-based Technologies and Systems are able to support their procurement.

Since for the purchase of **routine services** clear and precise specifications can easily be prepared, they can be purchased utilizing the same techniques used to buy commodities [Dobl1984, pp. 193-194]. Consequently, the supporting Internet based Technologies and Systems are the same than the ones for

125

commodities introduced in section 5.1. The procurement of routine services can be done/ supported through:

- Desktop purchasing systems (DPSs),
- Outsourcing strategies, and
- Sell-side solutions.

The focus of this section is on the procurement of **complex services**. The idea is to show how and if Internet based Technologies and Systems (IBTS) can support this type of purchase.

Complex services, as introduced in section 2.2.3.2 are characterized by being of high value, high risk, low transaction frequency, high complexity and low substitutability. Unlike routine services, standard specifications are unavailable when buying this type of service, thus, a unique and enforceable S.O.W. must be developed.

The nature of complex services, respectively the characteristics of them, need to be taken into consideration when looking for IBTS to support this type of procurement.

Most of the approaches presented in chapter 4 concentrate in reducing the cost of processing a purchase order (**transaction cost**) by automating the process and doing it electronically. This makes a lot of sense when purchasing commodities or routine services, characterized by a high transaction frequency and low cost. The savings obtained by lowering the transaction costs can be significant, due to the high transaction frequency. However, when considering buying complex services, which might be worth millions and are purchased only seldom, it does not make much sense to lower the transaction costs, because the transaction is done so rarely. Much bigger savings can be obtained by making the right purchase decisions, for example in choosing the appropriate supplier. If for example, two potential suppliers offer an equivalent service, but the difference in price is half a Million US-dollar a year, this difference translates directly into bottom line savings when making the right decision, where as when

concentrating on reducing the transaction costs, only a few hundred dollars go to the bottom line. Therefore, when looking for IBTS to support the procurement of complex services, only those should be taken into account, which allow to support the **decision making** process.

Since DPS were introduced in section 4.2.1 as buy-side applications that are especially suitable for the procurement of low value, high volume items and focus mainly in driving costs out of the procurement process (lower transaction cost), they don't qualify as a supporting technology for the procurement of complex services.

The action model introduced in section 4.4, in contrast, seems to offer interesting possibilities to support the decision making process when purchasing complex services. Therefore it will be analyzed more in detail in the following.

5.2.1 Online-Internet-Auction- a business model for the purchase of services

An auction was introduce in section 4.4 as a mechanism where buyer(s) and seller(s) come together to determine the price of an item.

Usually this model is especially useful when items can be specified easily and price is the only variable determining the purchase decision.

Since the purchase decision of services is much more complex and based upon more variable than just price (see section 3.2 Purchasing Services), the auction model seems not suitable to be used as a mechanism for this type of purchase at first.

However, if variables are eliminated in advanced, and price is left as the only variable, the auction model can be applied.

Exactly this approach is used by start up company Freemarkets, a buyer driven intermediary (see section 4.4.4), in order to purchase high value industrial products. Similarly to complex services, high value industrial products can't be purchased from suppliers just by considering price as the only variable.

Therefore, Freemarkets invites potential suppliers that are able to meet the buyer's requirements, to participate on a real-time online auction over the Internet and compete over price, only after having eliminated all other variables in advance.

Freemarkets's business model [see Jahn1998, pp. 50-56; Leig1998, pp. 62-66] will be used in the following section to show how complex services could be purchased using a real-time online auction over the Internet to bring buyers and sellers together.

As of today, there seems to be no real case implementation that makes use of this type of approach in order to purchase complex services. The following description therefore has to be taken just as an idea of how the purchase of complex services could look like when trying to use an online auction over the Internet to support this type of procurement.

5.2.1.1 Procurement process support and change

In section 3.2 the procurement process for purchasing complex services was presented as a sequence consisting of several steps. The process begins with the definition of need, and ends with the pre-award conference. Figure 32 shows the purchasing process of complex services as it was introduced in section 3.2.

Figure 32: Purchasing process of complex services

In the approach presented in the following, three different market players participate in this purchasing process and need to be considered. They are:

- A **buyer** (or buying team), who defines the need and decides to purchase a service,

- an **intermediary**, who acts on behalf of the buyer and hosts the real time online auction over the Internet, and

- **potential suppliers**, who battle for the business.

The real time online Internet auction is the central part of this approach. It is preceded by a pre-auction off-line phase, and ends with a follow-up off-line phase as shown in Figure 33.

1. In the **pre-auction offline phase** the Intermediary works with the buying company to define a clear, accurate, and complete SOW and with potential suppliers which are able to meet these requirements. This phase ends, once equivalent good offers from suppliers are identified and all variables, except for price are eliminated

2. In the **real time online auction over the Internet** (or Extranet), potential suppliers compete over price (bid over price).

3. In the **follow up offline phase** the Intermediary supports the buyer in the pre-award conference.

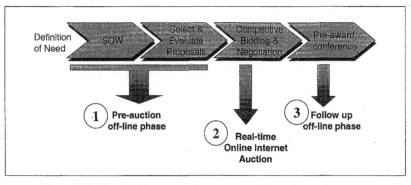

Figure 33: Auction & Bidding support the procurement of complex services

In the following, each of the three phases is going to be explained more in detail.

The entire **pre- auction off-line phase** is used to match the buyer's requirements (SOW) with different offers from potential suppliers. The idea is to

129

eliminate all variables, except for price, before inviting the most promising suppliers to the online auction. Therefore, the intermediary has to work with both buyer and suppliers:

1. Working with the **buyer**: The Intermediary works with the buyer's procurement organization personally, over the phone and over the Internet to define a clear, accurate and complete SOW. This step is critical to the success of this approach, since the SOW plays a key role in the procurement of complex services. All offers submitted by the supplier are measured against the SOW.

2. Working with **suppliers**: The intermediary identifies potential suppliers by asking for recommendations from the buyers themselves and by conducting research in catalogs and on the Web. Once a stable of potential suppliers has been assembled, the intermediary contacts each one of them and describes in detail what is wanted. Interested suppliers fill out questionnaires with precise information about their offering. Vendors (suppliers) that appear to meet the buyer's requirements are then subject to a more in depth analysis. Only the most promising ones, with equivalent offers, are then considered to take part in the next phase.

The pre-auction phase is over, once there has been a match between the buyer's SOW and the offers submitted by the service providers. All variables, expect for price, have been eliminated.

The most promising suppliers, able to meet the buyer's requirements, are then invited on a specific day and time to participate on the **real-time online Internet auction** that is hosted by the intermediary. Here they will battle over price by undercutting their competitors offer in order to get hold of the business. The suppliers will see its competitors' bids on a computer monitor, but the competitors will not be identified. Once the online auction is over, the lowest bidder will not necessarily be the one that is awarded the contract. This will be decided in the **pre-award conference** that is held off-line after the auction. Here the buyer meets with the intermediary to review all submitted offers again. Now, when the battle over price is completed and even the last variable is determined, it is easy to make the right decision and choose among the best offer that was submitted.

5.2.1.2 Consequences

Using this approach to purchase complex services has consequences for both buyers and suppliers.

Buyers gain buying power because:

1. They are able to enter the negotiation with much better information and

2. They have a mechanism that allows them to put suppliers into direct competition with one another making use of on-line auctions.

The purchasing decision of complex services is therefore improved. Other then that, this model does not come along with any significant organizational or personal changes within the buying company.

Sellers (supplier) loose power because they are not able to hide behind relationships anymore, but rather are put into direct competition with equally good supplier's. Due to the connectivity of the Internet, eventually these supplier are spread all over the world.

However the most interesting aspect of this new business model, which makes use of web-technology to bring buyers and sellers together, is the fact that suppliers fight over price in real-time online auctions. This means, that a mechanism is available which allows an exchange of prices and therefore is able to determine the real market value of an offer. Consequently the era of **fixed pricing** may be nearing, because Internet Technology is used to allow variable pricing [Jahn1998, pp. 50-56].

5.2.1.3 Limitations, Problems, and Requirements

The auction approach presented before might be useful to support the procurement of complex services, however it comes along with certain limitations, problems, and requirements that need to be taken into consideration:

131

1. The Buyer has to know exactly what he wants when defining the SOW. Often this is only possible after intensive conversations with potential suppliers.

2. When considering a service provider not only "hard-facts" are important, but especially the "chemistry" ("soft-facts") and confidence between buyer and seller are key aspects that influence the decision among different potential suppliers.

3. There has to be a **competitive supply market** with five or more viable suppliers that are able to meet the buyer's requirements in order to make use of the auction mechanism. If they are not in place, the online auction can't be carried out reasonable.

4. Suppliers and buyer must be willing and able to participate in this very new approach, which requires a certain openness to new technology and new business models.

5. The contract value has to be significantly high, in order to attract potential suppliers to participate.

6. The contract value and the potential savings must be significantly high in order to pay off for the involvement of an intermediary responsible for the online-auction.

5.3 Procurement of Information Technology

The distinction between hardware and software introduced in chapter 3.3 will be retained unchanged in this section for the procurement of IT. Support through Internet based technology and systems will be analyzed in the following for the procurement of both, hardware and software.

5.3.1 Hardware

The objective of this section is to analyze the support of IBTS, introduced in chapter 4, for the procurement of hardware. In section 3.3.3, hardware was defined as the physical aspects of computers and other information technology

devices. It includes not only the personal computers (PC) and laptops, but also peripheral devices such as keyboard, mouse, audio speakers and printers.

Hardware (in connection with software) can be considered a strategic tool for the support of different business functions. Therefore, purchasing personnel is acquiring hardware on regular bases to not only equip personnel, but also to keep up with technology updates. However, purchasing hardware is no routine task, because several aspects have to be considered. New devices need to be compatible with existing hardware, standards have to be met, and more than just acquisition cost need to be considered (refer to section 3.3.1 for more details on acquisition cost and hardware requirements). These considerations and requirements as well as the ability to configure the item make hardware procurement complex. Furthermore, different persons are involved in the decision to purchase. As discussed in section 3.3.2, end-users, purchasing and finance personnel and IT specialist are involved in the procurement process and therefore make the acquisition a team effort.

Now, that the key aspects of hardware procurement from chapter 3.3.3 are briefly outlined the IBTS from chapter 4 will be analyzed regarding if and how they support the procurement of hardware. The main idea is to look at **two** different scenarios:

1. In the **first scenario** - which will be outlined more in detail in section 5.3.1.1 – the assumption is that a procurement system with proper IT-tools to support the buying of indirect goods is already in place. An example would be an organization, which has implemented a DPS for the procurement of indirect goods and is now expanding the use of the system to purchase hardware. The task is to integrate hardware items in the existing electronic catalog and make them available for the end-users.

2. In the **second scenario** – which will be outlined more in detail in section 5.3.1.2 – the assumption is that **no** procurement system to support the purchase of indirect goods exists and organizations are looking for possibilities to support the procurement of hardware.

Looking at the IBTS outlined in chapter 4, outsourcing services and supplier sell-side solution seem to provide potential support for the procurement. Outsourcing services turn the responsibility of procurement to a third party and sell-side solutions offer end-users access to electronic catalogs that are hosted by the supplier.

Auction models were analyzed as a mechanism to purchase goods where price is the only variable for the buying decision. Therefore, it is difficult to take requirements such as standards, compatibility, and after sales service into consideration. Furthermore, they do not support the procurement process by empowering the end-user to purchase goods. Therefore they will not be of importance regarding the procurement of hardware.

After analyzing the support of desktop-purchasing systems (DPS) in section 5.3.1.1 as well as outsourcing services and sell-side solutions (see section 5.3.1.2) for the procurement of hardware, a brief conclusion will be provided in section 5.3.1.3.

5.3.1.1 First scenario: DPS support for the procurement of hardware

The assumption of the first scenario is that a procurement system with proper IT-tools to support the buying of indirect goods is already in place. A DPS was outlined as an example, which integrates an electronic catalog as the key element of the system. All products that are purchased through the system have to be included in this catalog. Therefore, hardware items have to be enclosed in the catalog as well. The problem is that hardware can be customized for a person's need. Therefore, catalogs will have to provide configuration tools. This problem will be discussed in **case one**.

An alternative to provide configuration tools is to eliminate the configuration problem up-front, by including only pre-configured and standardized devices into the catalog. This assumption is the premise for **case two**.

Now, in the following the possible support and deriving problems of a DPS solution for the procurement of hardware will be analyzed. First, case one will be discussed where a configuration tool is necessary and then case two will be analyzed, where standardized hardware devices are included in the catalog.

- **Case one:** In this case end-users purchase items with the support of a desktop-purchasing system. As outlined in section 3.1.3, the process starts with the definition of need by end-users who search in electronic catalogs, which are integrated in the system. These electronic catalogs turned out as the key factor of the system, which especially support the integration and selection of standardized items.

  Hardware however, is a complex item, which can be customized regarding to the requirements of the end-user. This means the requester can configure the product to meet his needs. The problem is that as of today, there are no configuration tools available that support the procurement of complex items such as hardware. This seems to be one of the main weaknesses of DPS right now [Sege1998]. Therefore, hardware has to be included in the catalog as a standardized, non-configurable item, which is the assumption of case two.

Case two: In this case hardware products, which can be selected from the electronic catalog, are already **pre-configured** (standardized) by the IT-department. The problems of configuration, standards, and compatibility are already addressed by a team of IT and purchasing personnel, before the items are placed in the catalog. In this case the end-user can choose only among certain types of standardized products. The purchasing process in this case will then be similar to purchasing commodities outlined in section 3.1.3.

Important here is that IT personnel decide upon the standards of the hardware before the items are placed in the catalog and are accessible by the end-users.

Using the system for purchasing standardized hardware products initiates similar changes for the purchasing personnel and the end-users as buying commodities. Refer to chapter 5.1.1.3 for organizational and personal changes in the case of buying commodities through a DPS.

5.3.1.2 Second scenario: Outsourcing services and sell-side solutions for the procurement of hardware

The assumption of the second scenario is that no procurement system to support the purchase of indirect goods exists. Therefore, organizations are looking for potential solutions to support the procurement of hardware. Two solutions have been selected in the second scenario. **Outsourcing services**, which will be analyzed first and **supplier sell-side solutions**, which will be analyzed second for their procurement support.

Outsourcing services: Outsourcing was defined in section 4.3 as transferring the responsibility of activities to a third party provider. For the procurement of hardware, this indicates that the outsourcer is in charge of buying, delivering and implementing the hardware equipment. Furthermore, the service provider is responsible for maintenance and service.

An organization seems to have the option to either buy or lease the equipment from the outsourcer. In case of leasing, additional equipment will be included in the leasing contract. Outsourcing of hardware equipment will provide an organization with several advantages:

One advantage of outsourcing hardware is that the buying organization will receive the expertise, focused knowledge and skill sets of the third-party service provider. Unless purchasing hardware is one of the buying organization's core competencies it will gain efficiency and receive faster process transaction. By relaying on the third party provider to keep up with changing technology (upgrades) and day-to-day operations of hardware the buying organization's purchasing personnel will be able to focus on different, more strategic tasks. Furthermore problems of standards, compatibility, system breakdown, service and maintenance are all in the hands of the provider.

An additional advantage is that outsourcing takes over human resource issues. Sourcing individuals with sound technology skills is difficult and expensive. The burden of screening, hiring and training these people is shifted to the third party.

Next, the impact on supplier sell-side solutions for the procurement of hardware will be analyzed.

Sell-side-solution: Supplier sell-side solutions have been introduced in chapter 4.1.1.1 as electronic product catalogs that are offered by suppliers at their own Web site. Sell-side solutions have the advantage that they support the configuration of complex items such as hardware. One example is the computer manufacturer DELL who provides an online electronic catalog. Buyers can connect via Internet (or Extranet) and have the possibility to search the catalog and configure their hardware device regarding their specific needs. Furthermore, the supplier offers services (e.g. support in case of failure) via e-mail or hotline for his customers.

As outlined in section 4.1.1.1, supplier sell-side solution can be separated in **public Web sites** that provide access for every person that is connected to the Internet, and **customized Web sites**, which can only be entered from buyers with access rights.

Public Web sites can be accessed by any end-users of an organization. They have the advantage that once the end-users have entered the electronic catalog they can select any device regarding to their specific needs. The disadvantages are on the side of the buying organization:

- They cannot control standards, configuration, compatibility or spending limits.

- They cannot make their business rules & policies valid for the requisitioner.

- They cannot leverage their purchase orders and therefore buy in high volumes and take advantage of volume discounts. Consequently, they do not have buying power.

- They cannot buy from preferred suppliers and make use of contract offers.

In order to address most of these problems, suppliers offer their business customers customized Web sites.

Customized web sites can only be accessed by end-users with password rights. The content of these electronic catalogs is specifically customized for the needs of their business customers. Therefore, end-users can only order pre-configured devices with specific qualities. Customized Web sites offer several advantages for their business customers:

- They only offer standardized devices and therefore problems of compatibility can be solved up-front.

- End-users order contract items with pre-negotiated items. Volume discounts can be used.

- Supplier provide data for the buying organization to create spending patterns.

- Business rules & policies can be integrated and therefore valid for any requisitioner.

- Catalog and content management is the responsibility of the supplier (vendor).

Overall, organizations have the ability to control their end-users, ensure that only certain devices are purchased, buy from preferred suppliers only and increase their buying power.

5.3.1.3 Conclusion

Resulting from the analysis of purchasing hardware with the support of DPS and supplier sell-side solutions, electronic catalogs seem to be the key issue. Integrated in a purchasing system (catalog at the buyer-side) electronic catalogs demand standardized products, since the configuration of items made up of a number of different components is not supported yet. This is the advantage of customized Web sites, which provide not only the configuration of hardware devices but also integrate customer's business rules & policies. Overall, as of today the customized sell-side catalogs and outsourcing services (regardless of leasing or buying the products) seem to meet best the requirements of hardware procurement.

5.3.2 Software

The main purpose of this section is to show if and how Internet-based Technology and Systems can support and might change the way in which organizations purchase software. Note though, that a company does not actually purchase software, but rather acquires "rights to use" software. Therefore software license agreements become critical, when considering the utilization of software (see section 3.3.4).

The differentiation into standard software and complex software introduces earlier in this thesis will be maintained throughout this section. The focus however is going to be on the procurement of **complex software**, such as ERP-, Electronic Commerce-, Database-, and Email applications, associated usually with high implementation and maintenance cost. For this type of software an emerging Internet business model has the potential to redefine the way in which organizations handle software [Fole1998].

Nevertheless, the Internet does offer some interesting possibilities that support and change the way in which low cost, low risk **standard software** can be purchased. Software stores and vendors are available online and offer a huge variety of "out of the box" software products that can be purchased electronically. Those products are downloaded instantly over the Internet straight into the end-users computer. Normally online payment is also supported. In this case the whole purchasing cycle is done electronically, from information and sourcing of products to delivery and payment. Since this type of purchases does impact especially on the business-to-consumer segment, it is not going to be explained any further in this thesis.

The emerging Internet business model that could change the way in which organizations acquire **complex software** is currently associated with a variety of definitions and terminology's; the most common ones are: Web-hosting, application outsourcing, web-based application outsourcing, networked-based hosted applications, Application Service Providers (ASPs), software rental and software lease.

In the following the term "web based application outsourcing" will be used, because it seems to describe best the idea of this new approach.

The main idea behind this business model is to host and manage complex software applications in remote locations, instead of implementing them within a company. By doing this, customers don't have to purchase expensive software and hardware to run specific applications, but can lease them from a third party which is responsible for the maintenance. Therefore the customer can derive the full value of an application without the burdens associated with the ownership.

Simply put, software vendors sell their applications to some third party (service provider), who in turn host and manage the software, and lease its use to organizations, usually on a user-per-month basis [Elgi1998]. In some cases the software vendor itself might host the application instead of a third party.

This is a fundamentally different way to sell software, because it mixes Electronic Licensing and Electronic Payment. The Internet and Electronic Licensing make it possible to sell access to software based on actual software use.

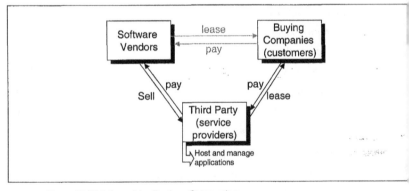

Figure 34: Web-based Applications Outsourcing

According to James Barksdale, Netscape Corporations Corp. CEO and President, **application outsourcing** will be the next growing trend, because the "networked economy" ends the need for data to reside in a specific physical location. Internet computing allows to have centralized application servers and database servers that can be shared by users around the world [Sim1998].

As of today it seems as though nearly every top independent software vendor is still struggling with their Web-hosting efforts and much uncertainty remains concerning this topic. Nevertheless, web hosting strategies have lately been announced by vendors such as SAP AG, Oracle Corp., People Soft Inc., The Baan Co., J.D. Edwards, Microsoft Corp., and Lotus Development Corp. They currently nearly outnumber the customers who are actually outsourcing applications through this new business model [Fole1999; Cald1998].

To what extend this innovative approach will impact the way in which customers buy software remains uncertain. Some analysts predict that application outsourcing will ultimately become the dominant model for how applications are delivered [Cald1998].

Due to the attention web-based application hosting is getting by mayor software vendors and the potential it might have in changing the way in which company's acquire software, it is going to be analyzed more in detail in the following.

5.3.2.1 Web-based application outsourcing

Web-based-application was introduced previously as a new approach for software vendors to distribute their products, and for buyers to acquire those applications. The concept is based on the idea that software applications no longer have to be implemented within a company, but can be hosted and managed by a third party, usually a so called Application Service Provider (ASP), in a remote location.

Many applications are already available and offered this way. Among them the most important ones are:

- Email applications

- Groupware & Videoconferencing applications

- Sales Force automation applications

- ERP applications

- Database applications

- Electronic Commerce applications, and

- Procurement applications, such as Desktop Purchasing Systems.

Most of these applications require significant infrastructure changes, lengthy and complex evaluation cycles, and skilled staff to implement and maintain the final customized solution. They usually come along with notable costs for consulting and integration services, which easily can exceed the cost of the actual software.

Therefore some necessary requirements for a successful implementation of this type of application are:

1. Enough and knowledgeable in-house IT-personnel,

2. Appropriate IT-Infrastructure (hardware & software), and

3. Sufficient financial resources to purchase those applications.

Traditionally, only the largest companies have been able to meet these requirements, leaving small and midsize companies excluded from the use of these applications.

With the possibility to host and manage these applications in a remote location and lease their use to interested customers, most of the obstacles that small and midsize companies have faced when considering to implement those applications can be addressed. The value proposition of application outsourcing is the following [Cald1998]:

- Reduce time and cost of implementation because hardware and software are already in place at the third party location.

- Reduce capital expenditures on hardware, because application and database servers are hosted and maintained by the third party.

- Avoid Software development, maintenance, and administration, because the application is updated and maintained by the outsourcer.

- Reduce fixed cost, because applications are rented instead of purchased.

Summarizing these points, the value lies in the fact, that a company can use applications, without the burdens associated with the ownership.

Therefore this model seems to be especially appealing and suitable for small and midsize companies interested in this type of applications, which used to be out of their price range. Early customers of web-based-application outsourcing tend to be small, startups, or company spin-offs that need access to business applications but don't want to invest in an internal IT structure.

Access to the remote application server is usually done through dedicated lines (T1 or ISDN). Oversimplified, an Internet connection and a recent Web browser are the only requirements to access those applications. However, as depict later in this section, other issues, such as security, need to be taken into account and are critical for the viability of this business model.

The way in which customers pay for the outsourcing service is still not defined yet. However, as the outsourcing channel matures, buyers will most likely get increasing options to choose from, ranging from [Buss1998]:

- Flat-fee access,

- To monthly service charges, and

- per-transaction pricing.

Even though this model seems to offer interesting new ways to acquire software, it comes along with several limitations and issues that need to be taken into account when a buyer considers outsourcing software applications. Some of them are shortly mentioned in the following:

1. This concept does not hold yet for every company. It is particularly targeted to small and medium size companies, that can't afford to invest heavily in Information Technology or don't have the IT capabilities and personnel to do so.

2. Application outsourcing is especially suitable for companies that don't need tailor-made solutions, but can make use of almost standardized "off-the-shelf" applications, with little need of adaptation. Therefore large companies usually don't qualify, because they need applications that are customized to their requirements.

3. Due to the strategic nature of complex software, outsourcing applications is involved with risk. Companies might hesitate to give up control of a strategic resource to a third party. Therefore security and trust become critical when considering this business model as an alternative way to acquire software.

Due to the immaturity of this business model, it is currently very difficult to predict the implications and changes that are most likely going to take place within the buying organization. It seems as though it does not come along with any significant changes for the procurement department, because it is just a new way to acquire software. Instead of license agreements, long term outsourcing agreements with service providers have to be managed and closely monitored, due to the strategic importance that most of these application represent. The IT-department might experience more important changes, which may help to relief the current IT-shortage, because less IT-personnel is needed in-house to manage, maintain, and administer the applications. However, it seems not to be a goal of service providers to replace the IT staff, but rather to work in conjunction with them [Elgi2].

In conclusion, each buying company has to evaluate for itself to which extend they embrace this new business model in order to "purchase"/ acquire software.

The Gartner Group for example predicts that by 2001, 65% of midsize enterprises will outsource some or all of their companies' mailboxes to a third party [Cox1999]. For the ERP market the outsourcing trend will represent just a single -digit percentage of the total ERP market within the next five years, which suggests that the traditional channels will dominate for this type of applications [Buss1998].

6 Conclusion

The objective of this thesis was to discuss if and how Internet-based technologies and systems (IBTS) are able to support the procurement of indirect goods and services.

Therefore, the thesis started in chapter 2 with an introduction of the fundamentals of procurement and a differentiation between direct and indirect procurement. In doing so, indirect procurement was identified as a long neglected area of procurement that had received little attention for efficiency gains, even though it is characterized as being complex, paper-based, and inefficient.

Since the procurement process and requirements for the wide range of indirect goods and services vary significantly according to the item's characteristics, a **clustering model** was introduced that allowed to identify different types of indirect procurement with similar requirements regarding the procurement process.

Based on the clustering model, six procurement types were identified and then analyzed more in detail in chapter 3, with regards to their special requirements to the procurement process. The six procurement-types are:

- Commodities (items of low value, high volume, and high frequency),
- routine and complex Services,
- standard and customized Software, and
- Hardware

The most significant inefficiencies in the procurement process were identified within the procurement type of commodities. The user requirements derived from the analysis demanded for driving costs out of the procurement process (reduce transaction costs), by simplifying and automating the procurement process.

In chapter 4 several **Internet-based Technologies and Systems** have been introduced with regards to their potential to support the procurement of indirect goods and services. The most promising solutions that were analyzed more in detail are:

- Desktop purchasing systems (DPS),

- Sell-side solutions (customized and non-customized),

- Outsourcing services ("traditional", IT-outsourcing, and innovative), and

- Auctions.

Utilizing the above listed IBTS a **matching** with the procurement types identified in chapter 3 was realized in Chapter 5. The objective was to analyze the potential support for the procurement processes and identify if and how the user requirements are met. This matching is depict in the figure below, where the analyzed IBTS are listed on the abscissa of the matrix whereas the ordinate shows the identified procurement types.

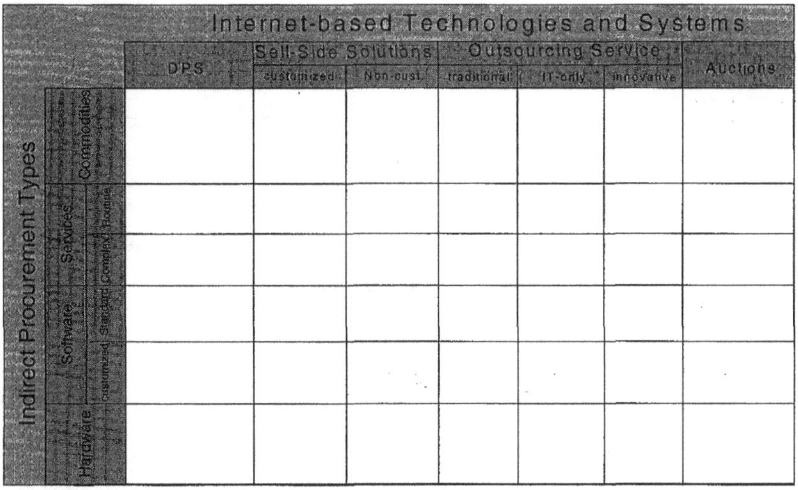

			Internet-based Technologies and Systems					
		DPS	Sell-Side Solutions		Outsourcing Service			Auctions
			customized	Non-cust.	traditional	IT-only	innovative	
Indirect Procurement Types	Commodities							
	Services							
	Software							
	Hardware							

Figure 35: Matching between procurement types and IBTS

This thesis analyzed all the possibilities (6x7=42) with regards to if and how Internet based Technologies and Systems are able to meet the special requirements of each procurement type. In addition, organizational changes, as well as existing weaknesses due to the implementation of Internet based Technologies were depict. The most interesting findings are briefly summarized in the following:

1. The most comprehensive solution to support the procurement type of **commodities** are desktop purchasing systems. These systems are based on electronic catalogs and offer a self-service user-friendly environment, which empower the end-user to execute the actual buying. This helps to free the purchasing department from day-to-day procurement transactions and allow it to focus on more strategic value adding tasks.

   On the other side, DPS demand significant customization efforts and implementation cost. Furthermore, new responsibilities such as catalog and content management, as well as integration difficulties with back-end systems arise. Therefore, as of today they are especially suitable for large companies with sufficiently inefficient procurement processes.

2. Online auctions over the Internet were introduced as a possibility to support the procurement of **complex services**. They allow putting potential suppliers into direct competition and therefore reduce the cost of the item purchased.

3. An emerging Internet business model, called Web-based application outsourcing was introduced and explained, because it has the potential to significantly change the way in which organizations acquire **complex software.** The idea is to host and manage complex software applications in remote locations, instead of implementing them within a company. This is possible, because the "networked economy" ends the need for data to reside in a specific physical location.

4. The procurement of **hardware**, which needs to consider standards and compatibility issues among others, is currently best supported by customized sell-side solutions. These catalogs, implemented at the supplier side, can only be accessed by authorized (password, login) end-users. The advantage is, that purchasing and IT personnel can appoint the content of the catalog in a team effort. Therefore, the end-user searching the catalog will only be able to

histories and usage statistics in an easy-to-understand format. Procurement and financial professionals should be able to monitor internal budgets and vendor performance. Finally, detailed information on items purchased should be available for use during future negotiations with suppliers.

- **Ease of implementation and administration:** A buy-side application should be easy to administer – the goal is to create less, not more work for the procurement, finance and other departments. A system should free professionals to focus on strategic supplier management, rather than tie them down with operational details.

- **Scalability:** A buy-side application should be able to grow (scalability) and accommodate increasing number of users and/ or functionalities as the necessity of this arises.

Besides these considerations, a **checklist** of features and functions regarding buy side applications is provided as an Appendix in this thesis (see Appendix 1 at page 157). This checklist was requested from *American Tech* (www.purchasingnet.com), a software vendor in the area of purchasing & requisitioning systems, and allows to select and justify buy-side procurement applications.

4.3 Outsourcing

Outsourcing has become a very popular management option in the last decade. Currently it accounts for only 1% of all expenses but it is expected to continue to grow at double-digit rates [Sege1998].

Outsourcing indicates transferring responsibility of activities to a third party, which used to be performed internally. That third party is generally a supplier or a specialized intermediary [Ellr, 1997]. This is equal to taking an operation or function traditionally performed in house and moving it out to a contract manufacturer or third party service provider [Morg, 1998].

A significant push supporting the growing outsourcing trend is associated with the increasing use of Internet related Technologies, such as Internet, Intranet and Extranet, connecting buyers, sellers, and intermediaries around the world. In this "networked" economy new outsourcing business models and new outsourcing strategies are emerging and have the potential to redefine in certain areas the traditional outsourcing question regarding "make" or "buy". Especially regarding the acquisition of complex business applications, such as Enterprise Resource Planning (ERP) systems, some interesting new outsourcing possibilities are emerging.

Before explaining some "traditional" and "new" outsourcing business models in the area of procurement in section 4.3.3, an overview of the most common reasons for outsourcing business functions or certain goods and services will be depict (see section 4.3.1) and different degrees of outsourcing (see section 4.3.2) introduced.

4.3.1 Reasons for outsourcing

Traditionally, resources necessary to carry out business processes such as, labor, power, materials, machines, information and energy had be leased, owned or rented. In recent years, however, many organizations experience that some resources under their control are not performing as well as those that they could obtain from outside the company. In addition, outsourcers have the expertise and economies of scale to provide services at the same or higher quality level than the purchasing firm and at a lower total cost [Dobl, 1996, p. 409]. Therefore more and more companies decide to outsource resources if they can be obtained at better quality and/or lower cost from outside the company. They are looking for suppliers who are best in a field and who are able to perform business operations faster, better and cheaper in areas where they are weak [Morg, 1998]. Among common outsourced resources are cleaning services, lawn care and auto fleet management and even whole business processes like the procurement of certain items. The main idea is to own, nature and concentrate only on the core choose upon pre-selected items with pre-negotiated prices. This way the end-user is able to configure the hardware device regarding his needs and simultaneously ensure compatibility and standard of the ordered device.

Summarizing it can be stated that currently low value, high volume items (e.g. commodities) are the "**low hanging fruit**". For this procurement type, Internet based Technologies and Systems are easiest to implement and promise the biggest returns. Several buying companies have realized this fact, and are currently starting to embrace these solutions in order to support the procurement of commodities. Nevertheless, this thesis showed how also other than these low cost, high volume items can be supported by Internet based Technologies and Systems.

References

AMR (1997) Advanced Manufacturing Research. "The Report on Supply Chain Management - Defining The Future of Supply Chain Management Systems". Report. July 1997.

Agentics (1998) Agentics: Distributed-catalog Integration for E-commerce – White Paper. http://www.agentics.com/pages/whitepaper.html

Aspect Development (1998) Aspect Development. "MRO Catalog Products - Electronic Business-to-Business Purchasing". White Paper. 1998.

Avery, Susan (1997, Jan. 16) Avery, Susan: License agreements add value to buy, Purchasing Magazine, January 16, 1997

Avery, Susan (1997, June 19) Avery, Susan: Thinking of outsourcing?, Here is what to consider..., Purchasing magazine, June 19, 1997

Avery, Susan (1998, Nov. 5) Avery, Susan: Mergers put spotlight on supplier capability, Purchasing Magazine, November 5, 1998

Avery, Susan (1998, Sep. 15) Avery, Susan: Leverage doesn't end when the agreement is signed, in Purchasing Magazine, September 15, 1998

Baan (1998) Baan Company N.V. "Baan Concepts: Supply Chain Management". http://www.baan.com/solutions/Concepts/supply/-supbroc.htm (06/28/98).

Beam, Carrie (1998) Beam, Carrie; Segev, Arie: Auctions on the Internet: A field study, November 1998

Berryman et al.(1998) Berryman, Kenneth; Harrington, Lorraine; Lazton-Rodin, Dennis and Rerolle, Vince: *Electronic Commerce: Three emerging strategies.* The McKinsey Quarterly 1998, Number 1.

Bouverie-Brine, C. (1995) Bouverie-Brine, Christopher & Nick Rich: Cross-Functionality, Organizational Decision Making & the role of purchasing – procurement of an IT Systems by London Underground Limited, in: Advanced Supply Management edited by Andrew Cox (1997), p. 255-297

Buchanan (1997) Buchanan, Leigh. "Procurative Powers". In: *WebMaster Magazine.* May 1997. http://www.cio.com/archive/webbusiness/ 050197_procurement_content.html (07/01/98).

Burt, David N. (1984)	Burt, David: Proactive Procurement – The key to increased profits, productivity, and quality – A Step by step procedural guide to move from a reactive purchasing activity to a proactive profit-making procurement system, New Jersey, 1984
Burt, David N. (1990)	Burt, David N.;Norquist, Warren E.; Anklesaria, Jimmy: Zero Base Pricing – Achieving Word Class Competitiveness through reduced all-in-cost, Probus Publishing Company, Chicago, IL, 1990
Busse, Thorsten (1998)	Busse, Thorsten: ERP outsourcing options coming to your neighborhood, in: InfoWorld Electric, September 1, 1998, http://-www.infoworld.com/cgi-bin/displayStory.pl?98091.woutsoruce.-html
Byles, Torrey (1999)	Byles, Torrey: Electronic Catalog Alert, Volume 2, No. 1, Granada Research 1999, http://www.granadaresearch.com
Caffrey, Brian (1997)	Caffrey, Brian: Electronic Catalogs, in: The mining company, March 31, 1997, http://purchasing.miningco.com/library/weekly-/aa021299.htm
Caffrey, Brian (1998)	Caffrey, Brian: Blanket orders; the mining company, http://purchasing.tqn/library/weekly/aa032098.htm
Caldwell, Bruce (1998)	Caldwell, Bruce: Application Outsourcing – Web-Host Appeal, in: Information Week, 21/28 Dec. 1998, http://www.-informationweek.com/714/14iuhos.html
Carter, Narasimhan (1995)	Carter, Joseph R. and Ram Narasimhan. *Purchasing and Supply Management: Future Directions and Trends.* Center for Advanced Purchasing Studies, Arizona State University Research Park. Tempe, AZ. 1995.
Chadwick, Rajagopal (1995)	Chadwick, Tom and Shan Rajagopal. *Strategic Supply Management: An Implementation Toolkit.* Oxford, United Kingdom: Butterworth-Heinemann Ltd. 1995.
Chapman, T.L. et al. (1997)	Timothy L. Chapman, et al.: Purchasing: No time for lone rangers, in: The McKinsey Quarterly, 1997 Number 2, pp. 30 – 40
CommerceNet (1998)	CommerceNet: "Catalog Interoperability Study: Issues, Practices, & Recommendations". Research Report. Study

	Conducted for the Federal Electronic Commerce Program Office and the Interagency Acquisition Internet Council. February 27, 1998. http://www.commerce.net/research (07/01/98).
Cox, Nancy (1998)	Cox, Nancy: Are you outsourcing E-Mail?, in: Information Week, November 16, 1998, http://www.informationweek-.com/709/09iuout.html
CUPG (1985)	CUP GUIDANCE, Central Unit on Purchasing, No. 39 Basic Purchasing and Supply, p.2
Dempsey, Jed et al. (1997)	Dempsey, Jed et al.: Escaping the IT abyss – Information Technology/ Systems, in: Mckinsey Quarterly 1997, Number 4, pp. 81-91.
Dempsey, Jed et al. (1998)	Dempsey, Jed et al.: A hard and soft look at Information Technology, in: Mckinsey Quarterly 1998, Number 1, pp. 127-137.
Dobler, Burt (1996)	Dobler, Donald W. and David N. Burt. *Purchasing and Supply Management - Text and Cases.* Sixth Edition. New York, NY: McGraw-Hill. 1996.
Dobler, Donald W. (1984)	Dobler, Donald W.; Lee, Lamar Jr.; Burt, David N.: Purchasing and the Materials Management – Text and Cases, Forth Edition, McGraw-Hill Book Company, 1984
Dolberg, Stan (1998)	Dolberg, Stan: Sizing Commerce Software, Forrester Report, Commerce Technology Stragegies, Vol. 1, No. 1, May 1998
Elgin, Ben (1998)	Elgin, Ben: Oracle: The Latest Software Rental Advocate, August 26, 1998, http://www.zdnet.com/sr/breaking/-980824/980826d.html
Elgin, Ben (1998)	Elgin, Ben: Come and get it – Software for Rent, in Zdnet, March 9, 1998, http://www.zdnet.com/sr/breaking/980309/980309a.html
Ellram, Lisa (1997)	Ellram, Lisa: Outsourcing: Implications for supply management, Center for advanced purchasing studies, 1997
Färber, Frank (1998)	Färber, Frank: Internet Commerce Applications for the Procurement of Indirect Goods and Services; Diplomarbeit (master thesis), Technische Universitaet Darmstadt, Fachbereich Rechts- und Wirtschaftswissenschaften, August 1998

Fearon et al. (1993)   Fearon, Harold E. and Donald W. Dobler, Kenneth H. Killen (Eds.). *The Purchasing Handbook*. Fifth Edition. New York, NY: McGraw-Hill, Inc. 1993.

Feldman, Michael D. (1999)   Feldman, Michael D.: The Art of the Software Deal, in National Association of Purchasing 1999. http://www.napm.org/NewsAnd-Resources/artofthesoftwaredeal.cfm

Foley, Mary Jo (1999)   Foley, Mary Jo: Move over ISPs, here come the ASPs, February 16, 1999, http://www.zdnet.com/sr/stories/issue/0,4537,349557,-00.html

Gebauer et al. (1998)   Gebauer, Judith and Carrie Beam, Arie Segev. "Impact of the Internet on Procurement". Submitted to Acquisition Review Quarterly. February 1998. http://haas.berkeley.edu/~citm/-procurement/intro.html (07/08/98).

Gebauer, Judith (1996)   Gebauer, Judith : Informationstechnische Unterstützung von Transaktionen - Eine Analyse aus ökonomischer Sicht, Wiesbaden/Germany 1996.

Goeffrey, Moore (1999)   Moore, Geoffrey: The dearth of online catalogs is holding back e-commerce, in: Red herring magazine, Feb. 1999.

Heinritz, Stuart et al (1991)   Heinritz, S. et al: Purchasing, Principles and Applications, 8 th. Edition, 1991

Hough, Ashley (1992)   Hough, Harry E. and James M. Ashley. *Handbook of Buying and Purchasing Management*. Englewood Cliffs, NJ: Prentice Hall. 1992.

Jahnke, Art (1998)   Jahnke, Art: How Bazaar, in: CIO Web Business, Section 2, August 1, 1998

Killen & Associates (1997)   Killen & Associates. "Operating Resources Management: How Enterprises Can Make Money by Reducing ORM Costs". White Paper. Second Quarter, 1997.

Killen, Kenneth H. (1995)   Killen, Kenneth H. and John W. Kamauff: *Managing Purchasing: Making the Supply Team Work*. Volume 2 of the NAPM Professional Development Series. New York, NY: McGraw-Hill. 1995.

Koch, Nora (1997)   Koch, Nora; Mandel, Luis: State of the Art and Classification of

	Electronic Product Catalogs on CD-Rom, in: International Journal of Electronic Markets, University of St. Gallen Switzerland, Vol. 7, No. 3, 1997
Kotler, Philip (1997)	Kotler, Philip: Marketing Management, Analysis, Planning, Implementation, and Control. Ninth Edition, 1997
Kraljic, P (1983)	Kraljic, P: *Purchasing must become Supply Management* In: Harvard Business Review September-October 1983
Lee, H.G. (1996)	Lee, H.G.: electronic brokerage and electronic auction: The impact of IT on market structures, in J. F. Nunamaker and R. H. Sprague (eds), Proceedings 29th HIICS, Vol. IV: Information Systems – organizational Systems and technology, IEEE Computer Society Press, Los Alamitos, CA, pp.397 – 406
Leigh, Buchanan (1998)	Leigh, Buchanan: Seller door, in: Inc. Tech, September 15, 1998, pp. 62-66
Lincke, David-M. (1997)	Lincke, David-Michael: Evaluating Integrated Electronic Commerce Systems; University of St.Gallen, Switzerland
Minahan, Tim (1998)	Minahan, Tim: Enterprise Resource Planning: Strategies not included, in: Purchasing Magazine, July 16, 1998
Morgan, Jim (1998)	Morgan, Jim: The great outsourcing push!, Purchasing Magazine, March 26, 1998
Nissen, Mark E (1996).	Knowledge-Based Reengineering: From Mysterious Art to Learnable Craft, Fisher Center for Information Technology and Management, University of California at Berkeley, Working Paper 96-WP-1012, February 1996
Perlman (1990)	Perlman, Kalman I. *Purchasing and Materials Management.* Chicago, IL: Probus Publishing Company. 1990.
Porter, Anne Millen (1993)	Porter, Anne Millen: Tying down total costs, in: Purchasing, October 21, 1993
Porter, M. Anne (1997)	Porter, M. Anne: Buyers to third party purchasers: 'Get lost!', Purchasing Magazine, Sept. 14, 1997
Porter, M.E. (1985)	Competitive Advantage, Free Press: New York, 1985
Romm, Celia (1998)	Romm, Celia T.; Sudweeks, Fay: Doing Business Electronically,

A Global Perspective of Electronic Commerce, London 1998

Segev, Arie et al. (1998)   Segev, Arie; Gebauer, Judith; Frank Färber: The market of Internet technology based systems for indirect procurement, (not published yet) Research Report from the Fisher Center for Management and Information Technology, Haas School of Business, University of California at Berkeley, October 1998

Seltzer, Larry (1999)   Selzter, Larry: Bidding Frenzy; online auctions, in: Purchasing Magazine, March 9, 1999

Shapiro (1998)   Shapiro, Steve: Plugging the Leaks. EC World. November 1998

Shapiro, Carl (1999)   Shapiro, Carl; Varian, Hal R.: Information Rules, a strategic guide to the networked economy. Harvard Business School Press, Boston Massachusetts, 1999

Sim, Philip (1998)   Sim, Philip: Application outsourcing next trend, Barskdale says, in: Computerworld, August 28, 1998, http://www.computer-world.com/home/news.nsf/all/9808285appout

Solish, Fred (1998)   Solish, Fred: It's time to try transactional processing, http://www.ebnonline.com/tech/purch

TPN (1999)   TPN Register: Content Management: Key to success of Internet Procurement of Non-Production Supplies, White Paper, TPN Register LLC, http://www.tpnregister.com

Vigoroso, Marc (1998)   Vigoroso, Marc: Success depends on much more than supplier pick, in: Purchasing Magazine, 1998

Vigoroso, Mark (1998)   Vigoroso, Mark: Success depends on much more than supplier pick, in: Purchasing Magazine, 1998

Watts et al. (1998)   Watts, Charles A. and Kee Young Kim, Chan K. Hahn. "Linking Purchasing to Corporate Competitive Strategy". In: *International Journal of Purchasing & Materials Management*. Vol. 31, No. 2, Spring 1995: 3-8.

Webmethods   WebMethods: Business-to-Business E-commerce Solutions, by Anne Thomas, June 1998 http://www.webmethods.com/-products/b2b/b2b_wp.html

Wilder, Clinton (1997)   Wilder, Clinton: Web Site To Host Auction Of Surplus

Technology, in: Information Week Online, Sep. 15, 1997

Yankee (1998)   Yankee Group: Building an Electronic Employee Purchasing Solution Across the Internet, Internet Computing Strategies Report, Vol. 3., No. 13, October 1998

Yankee Group (1998)   Building an Electronic Employee Purchasing Solution Across the Internet, Internet Computing Strategies Report, Vol. 3., No. 13, October 1998

Zenz, Gary J.(1994)   Zenz, Gary J.: Purchasing and the Management of Materials, 7th ed., New York etc. 1994

Appendix 1

Features & Functions Checklist for Web-Based buy-side procurement applications.

(see 4.2.3 Evaluating Buy-Side Procurement Applications, page 87)

General

- ☐ Does the system include a back-office Purchasing System?
- ☐ How many installations are there?
- ☐ Can back-office reports be output to HTML and viewed with a browser?
- ☐ Can the workstations be Mac's, PC's, or Unix machines? (Platform independence)
- ☐ Does any part of the software have to be installed on the workstation?
- ☐ Does the system support a thin-client?
- ☐ Is the system N-Tier Client/Server Architecture?
- ☐ Does the system include both a browser and windows user-interface?
- ☐ Can the user create Ad-Hoc Reports?
- ☐ Are there any standard reports? How many?
- ☐ Can user "permissions" be established from a Group Profile?
- ☐ Can transactions be encrypted? (Security)
- ☐ Does the system support any browser? (Microsoft's and/or Netscape's)

Purchasing (Back-Office Component)

- ☐ Can the catalog be maintained by you or the supplier? How?
- ☐ Can supplier catalogs be downloaded electronically?
- ☐ Can supplier catalogs be translated then loaded?
- ☐ Can catalogs be searched by Commodity?
- ☐ Can catalogs be searched by Item Description?
- ☐ Does the system support keyword searches?

- ❏ Can catalogs be searched by Item Number?
- ❏ Can catalogs be searched by Preferred Supplier?
- ❏ Does the system contain Dollar Commitment and Price Analysis Reports?
- ❏ Can the system perform 2 way/3 way invoice matching?
- ❏ Can the user change business rules by Order Type?
- ❏ Does the system support a unit cost with 4 decimal places?
- ❏ Can data be imported/exported from the system? How?
- ❏ Can you update Master Tables "on-the-fly" while creating P.O.'s (Suppliers, Buyers, Ship-To, etc.)?
- ❏ Can you establish default values for P.O. fields?
- ❏ Does the system support Unlimited Item Description?
- ❏ Can you order items without Item Numbers?
- ❏ Does the system support attachments to P.O.'s and Requisitions?
- ❏ Does the system handle service orders?
- ❏ Does the system handle National Contracts?
- ❏ Does the system handle Blankets/Releases?
- ❏ Does the system handle RFQ's?
- ❏ Does the system handle P-Card orders?
- ❏ Does the system handle partial receipts?
- ❏ Does the system handle unplanned receipts?
- ❏ Does the system handle traditional P.O.'s? Can they be amended?
- ❏ Can you create P.O.'s without a Requisition?
- ❏ Does the system have a hold file for partially completed P.O.'s?
- ❏ Does the system assign P.O. numbers? Can they be overridden?
- ❏ Can you print variable footers on P.O. copies?
- ❏ Can the P.O. form be customized?
- ❏ Does the system contain User-Defined Fields?
- ❏ Can a P.O. be generated from a template P.O.?
- ❏ Can you send orders via FAX, E-Mail, or EDI?
- ❏ Can you reprint a Purchase Order?

- ❑ Can the system provide an audit trail of all transactions?
- ❑ Does the system have a browser-based receiving transaction?

Requisitioning

- ❑ Does the system support the "Administrator Model" of Requisitioning?
- ❑ Does the system employ the "shopping cart" metaphor?
- ❑ Does the system support Direct Ordering? Can Direct Orders be amended?
- ❑ Can a Requisitioner be blocked from ordering/requisitioning certain items?
- ❑ Can a Requisitioner be blocked from viewing/amending other requisitions?
- ❑ Can a Requisitioner use a template order?
- ❑ Can a Requisitioner mix dissimilar items on one Requisition?
- ❑ Can Requisitions automatically be assigned to Buyers?
- ❑ Does the system perform auto split/consolidate when Requisitions flow into the Purchasing Department?
- ❑ Can Requisitioners be restricted based on Dollar Amounts? How?
- ❑ Can fields be designated as Mandatory or Optional? Can they be validated?
- ❑ Can Requisition forms be reformatted?
- ❑ Can free-form Requisitions be created with unlimited Item Description?
- ❑ Can one Requisition contain items from different catalogs or suppliers?
- ❑ Can Requisition/Order status be performed via a browser?
- ❑ Can order status be displayed by Requisitioner, Supplier and Item?
- ❑ Are prior approvals time and date stamped?

Approvals/Workflow

- ❑ Can Requisitions be approved via a browser?
- ❑ Can approval notification be done via E-Mail?
- ❑ Does the system support an unlimited number of approval levels?
- ❑ Can the Requisition be routed based on account code?
- ❑ Can the Requisition be routed based on commodity?

- ❏ Can the Requisition be routed based on dollar limits?
- ❏ Can the Requisition be routed based on organizational hierarchy?
- ❏ Can you establish mandatory routings?
- ❏ Can you designate permanent alternate approvers?
- ❏ Can you designate temporary alternate approvers?   (Vacation, Business Travel, etc.)
- ❏ Can Requisitions be routed without a pre-defined routing (ad-hoc routing)?
- ❏ Can approvals be done by Req. Line or the total Requisition?
- ❏ Can the system alert an approver when a Requisition is pending?
- ❏ Can the users change their own passwords?

Other

- ❏ Is there a Contract Management capability?
- ❏ Is there an Invoice Matching capability?
- ❏ Is there an Inventory Control capability?
- ❏ Is there an Asset Tracking capability?
- ❏ Is there a Bar Code capability?
- ❏ Is there a Stock Requisitioning capability?
- ❏ Is there a Supplier Performance Rating capability?

Diplom.de

Wissensquellen gewinnbringend nutzen

Qualität, Praxisrelevanz und Aktualität zeichnen unsere Studien aus. Wir bieten Ihnen im Auftrag unserer Autorinnen und Autoren Wirtschafts-studien und wissenschaftliche Abschlussarbeiten – Dissertationen, Diplomarbeiten, Magisterarbeiten, Staatsexamensarbeiten und Studien-arbeiten zum Kauf. Sie wurden an deutschen Universitäten, Fachhoch-schulen, Akademien oder vergleichbaren Institutionen der Europäischen Union geschrieben. Der Notendurchschnitt liegt bei 1,5.

Wettbewerbsvorteile verschaffen – Vergleichen Sie den Preis unserer Studien mit den Honoraren externer Berater. Um dieses Wissen selbst zusammenzutragen, müssten Sie viel Zeit und Geld aufbringen.

http://www.diplom.de bietet Ihnen unser vollständiges Lieferprogramm mit mehreren tausend Studien im Internet. Neben dem Online-Katalog und der Online-Suchmaschine für Ihre Recherche steht Ihnen auch eine Online-Bestellfunktion zur Verfügung. Inhaltliche Zusammenfassungen und Inhaltsverzeichnisse zu jeder Studie sind im Internet einsehbar.

Individueller Service – Gerne senden wir Ihnen auch unseren Papier-katalog zu. Bitte fordern Sie Ihr individuelles Exemplar bei uns an. Für Fragen, Anregungen und individuelle Anfragen stehen wir Ihnen gerne zur Verfügung. Wir freuen uns auf eine gute Zusammenarbeit.

Ihr Team der Diplomarbeiten Agentur

Diplomica GmbH
Hermannstal 119k
22119 Hamburg

Fon: 040 / 655 99 20
Fax: 040 / 655 99 222

agentur@diplom.de
www.diplom.de